PRAISE

~~~~

"*Where the Water Meets the Sand* is a wrenchingly personal story of devastating loss. Richly detailed, brutally honest, and vulnerable, this memoir traces one woman's struggle to reclaim her belief in herself and in the world around her. Without hyperbole, Manning presents recollections that are simultaneously recognizable and unimaginable."

—Coleen Grissom, PhD,
Professor of English, Trinity University

"*Where the Water Meets the Sand* is a touching memoir showing the remarkable resilience of a young wife and mother fighting for order in her life, while her husband is fighting in Viet Nam—an ocean away. Tyra's true story will move you deeply, as she reaches deep inside herself to overcome unbelievable odds."

—Naomi Fisher, USAF Nurse Corps,
366th USAF Dispensary, Da Nang, RVN, 1970–1971

"Manning's clear, honest voice is unflinching. Her love story, though tragic, is uplifting and beautifully told. Scenes with her young husband make him so alive and real for the reader that his loss is heartbreaking. Themes of love, death, and redemption reoccur throughout, like waves washing to shore. Manning lives bravely, letting life do what it does. Despite the hardships she faced, she has made something beautiful out of pain. Her resilience is inspiring—her story exquisite and not to be missed."

—Lisa Shatto Glasgow, author and editor

Where *the* Water Meets *the* Sand

Where *the* *Water*

A MEMOIR

Meets *the* *Sand*

TYRA MANNING

GREENLEAF
BOOK GROUP PRESS

The names and identifying characteristics of persons referenced in this book, as well as identifying events and places, have been changed to protect the privacy of the individuals and their families.

Military terms follow Chicago Manual Style instead of Department of Defense guidelines.

Published by Greenleaf Book Group Press
Austin, Texas
www.gbgpress.com

Distributed by Greenleaf Book Group

For ordering information or special discounts for bulk purchases, please contact Greenleaf Book Group at PO Box 91869, Austin, TX 78709, 512.891.6100.

Design and composition by Greenleaf Book Group
Cover design by Greenleaf Book Group
Cover: abstract waves ©iStockphoto.com/epic11

Cataloging-in-Publication data is available.

Print ISBN: 978-1-62634-272-9

eBook ISBN: 978-1-62634-273-6

Part of the Tree Neutral® program, which offsets the number of trees consumed in the production and printing of this book by taking proactive steps, such as planting trees in direct proportion to the number of trees used: www.treeneutral.com

TreeNeutral®

Printed in the United States of America on acid-free paper

16 17 18 19 20 21 10 9 8 7 6 5 4 3 2 1

First Edition

For Larry and Laura

CONTENTS

~~~~~~~~

Dr. Tyra Manning personifies what Dr. Karl Menninger meant when he said, "Troubled people who receive good psychiatric care can become weller than well."

He meant that a psychiatric illness can smother a person's ability to think clearly, their creativity, and their ambition, and that good treatment can restore all of these to people who have been the recipient of quality care.

Dr. Manning has dedicated her life to the care and education of children, including her remarkable sensitivity to children who have suffered an early loss of a parent, beloved grandparent, or a significant member of their family.

I have known Dr. Manning for forty-five years, first when I was the social worker who was part of the psychiatric team that admitted her to the C.F. Menninger Memorial Hospital, later as the principal of my children's middle school, and as a mentor to my wife, who was an elementary school teacher and later a principal of several Topeka elementary schools.

I hope that the reader of this gripping book will go away with clearer appreciation that it was not only the armed services members who fought in Vietnam who became casualties of that war but also many loved ones at home who suffered as well.

Nolan Brohaugh, MSW
The Menninger Clinic, retired

ACKNOWLEDGMENTS

~~~~~~~~~~~~~~~~

M_y immense gratitude goes to my entire publishing team at Greenleaf Book Group, including Hobbs Allison, Elizabeth Barrett, Rachael Brandenburg, Diana Ceres, Lindsey Clark, Steven Elizalde, Corrin Foster, Jen Glynn, Ashley Jones, and Magdalene Thomas.

My creative and bold marketing team, Gardi Wilks and Nancy Ford of Wilks Communications, are organized and deliver state of the art marketing options. They are strategic, yet concise. I could not be more appreciative.

I also thank my first readers Naomi Fisher, Lisa Glasgow, and Jim Boland for their valuable feedback.

Special appreciation goes to writing coaches Bridget Boland, who has been on my team since 2006, and Jill Dearman, who helped me out of a creative slump. They both offered immense support and expertise.

Laura Hull and Marianne Turney tirelessly reviewed rough drafts for technical issues and content.

Joanne Trahanas has been an ongoing supporter of my book and graciously offered photographs she took of Larry's funeral at Arlington.

The residency awarded by the Ragdale Foundation provided a place and time with other writers and the encouragement I needed to write my memoir.

Tom Yarborough, Larry's comrade in Vietnam, has offered his friendship since we connected in 1993. His support for Laura and me has been ongoing. A published author in his own right, he checked my facts regarding the specifics of Larry's plane crash. I thank him for his immeasurable support.

The men who served with Larry in Vietnam and those who trained with him during pilot training at Reese Air Force Base, as well as personal friends and colleagues who attended Larry's funeral at Arlington, demonstrated that after thirty-five years, our country does not forget. Thank you.

My gratitude and appreciation goes to the entire Menninger Clinic staff and especially my house doctor and the hospital aide and friend who accompanied me to West Texas to attend Larry's first memorial service. A special thank you goes to Nolan Brohaugh, my intake social worker and outpatient counselor for alcoholism. The therapeutic specialists who taught my classes and the kind and concerned food service and housekeeping employees were all professional and consistent in their expectations and care. I owe them all my life.

Finally, for their proactive forward thinking I thank the Menninger family who pioneered the establishment of the Menninger Clinic in a time when the oppressive and sometimes cruel treatment of the mentally ill and their families was unimaginable. Though we have come a long way, the stigma is still great. Too many still suffer without treatment due to financial hardships or lack of treatment availability.

INTRODUCTION

For soldiers, sailors, airmen, and marines, wars are always painful and sometimes deadly. Unfortunately, in our country's history, it has become all too common—especially with the Vietnam War—to focus exclusively on tales of combat, political maneuvering, or anti-war protests. We tend to forget the war's tragic effects on the families and the gut-wrenching trauma they experienced while sending a father, husband, son, or brother across the ocean to fight and perhaps die.

Where the Water Meets the Sand is a unique book because it peels away the layers and digs deeply into the trials and tribulations, and the successes and failures of one American family coping on the home front during the most divisive war in America's history. Through the author's eyes—with no holds barred—you will experience an emotional roller coaster ride that will take your breath away. This powerful memoir will introduce the reader to a young air force family, to a renowned mental health clinic in Kansas, to the jungles of Laos where a courageous pilot flying a top secret mission meets his fate, to a board room in River Forest, Illinois, where a dedicated school district superintendent fulfills a dream and a promise, and to Arlington National Cemetery, where a thirty-five-year odyssey finally ends.

I first met the author in 1994, when it was my honor to escort her on her first trip to the Vietnam Wall. Standing before shiny black granite panel W5, line 120, we could see the name of Tyra's late husband, Larry, superimposed inside our own reflections. We both cried. I had served in Vietnam with her husband as a member of the super-secret Prairie Fire unit, a small group of United States Air Force forward air controllers who supported Special Forces teams on their dangerous missions behind enemy lines. Larry was one of the best. Over the past twenty years I've become a true admirer of the author—she is also one of the best. Like her husband, she has become not only a good friend, but also one of my heroes, full of incredible courage, extraordinary determination, and a passion for teaching and learning. Widowed at a young age with a baby daughter, the author overcame horrendous problems and demons that would have destroyed most people. In a remarkable journey, as her book candidly details, she persevered, earning a doctorate in education and becoming one of the nation's top school superintendents.

An extraordinary book that adds a critical chapter to the literature about military families and the Vietnam experience, *Where the Water Meets the Sand* serves as an inspirational roadmap for all of us. We would do well as a nation to heed the lessons and messages it contains. I would like to personally thank Tyra for her courage and honesty in bringing her amazing story to light, a story that reminds us what the true cost of war is, and who pays the price.

Tom Yarborough
Colonel, USAF (Ret)
Author of *Da Nang Diary* and *A Shau Valor*

ONE

~

July 1970

I awoke gently, having forgotten as I slept. My husband, Larry, was sleeping next to me in the trailer home we had purchased three days earlier. The unfamiliar room felt strange. It made me remember. *He's leaving today.* I squeezed my eyes shut and snuggled in as close to him as I could, careful not to wake him. The darkness of the early morning matched the gloom in my soul. In a few short hours, Larry would leave for Vietnam. I pulled the sheets over my eyes, as if I could hide from the day. How could I let him go? What if he didn't come home? One day, when I was nine years old, my father hadn't come home. *It's not the same*, I told myself. *Daddy was sick.* No matter how I tried to use logic to unravel the connection between my father's death and Larry's leaving, the two remained strung together in my thoughts like pearls of fear and dread. Until now, Larry's departure hadn't seemed real. Regardless, it was happening. My husband had volunteered to fly combat missions in Vietnam.

My brother, Rodney, had gone to Vietnam and returned. I tried to convince myself that Larry would, too, but the thought wasn't enough to console me. I got up, padded into the bathroom, and swallowed a tranquilizer.

As I slipped back into bed and cuddled close to Larry, he opened his eyes and smiled. "Today's the day." He sounded like a kid on Christmas morning. My husband had been counting down the days until he deployed, while I'd been marking them off with dread. I had vowed to support Larry's dream of flying planes as a United States Air Force fighter pilot. I didn't want him to know how distraught I felt as he prepared to leave for Vietnam. But the thought of losing the person I loved most, the one who made me feel safe and who loved me no matter what, was excruciating.

Larry hummed as he showered. I heard our fifteen-month-old daughter, Laura, stirring in her crib down the hall. I wanted to stay in bed, but time refused to stop no matter how hard I willed it. I had to get up and take Larry to the airport. I bathed Laura then dressed her in her cutest outfit, a blue and white checked dress with matching panties. Today was the last day Larry would see our daughter for a while. *Maybe forever.* I pushed that awful thought from my mind, trying to get through what I needed to do.

Seconds ticked by, synchronized with my heartbeat, a slow, steady drumroll announcing my husband's impending departure. I spoon-fed Laura toddler cereal and peaches. Larry shaved, dressed, and packed the last of his things. As he got ready to go, I had trouble controlling my thoughts. One minute, I flashed on a memory of my father gasping for air and asking for his nitroglycerin. Next, I imagined Larry's plane crashing in a fiery blaze. Despite my efforts to stay focused and finish feeding Laura, I grew more agitated with each passing moment.

I didn't tell Larry how afraid I was for him to go. I knew what flying meant to him, and because of what he meant to me, I didn't want to burden him. I wanted to ask him to stay, but I didn't dare. I finished feeding Laura. Larry loaded his luggage into the trunk then walked back to the front porch. He took Laura from me and carried her to the car, whispering, "I love you," as he blew softly in her ear. Squealing with delight, she wrapped her arms around his neck. Panic raged in me, yet I was eerily calm as I followed Larry and Laura to the car. My beloved husband's dream was coming true. I wasn't about to let him see how much it cost me.

This was the day Larry had imagined since he was a little boy growing up on air force bases in the United States and Japan. The two of us had watched every late night WWI and WWII air combat movie we could find on television. We'd seen most of them twice. Larry reminded me of the young pilots in the movies. His blond hair and blue eyes made him appear younger than his twenty-four years. But this was not the movies. This was my husband, Laura's father. When a young pilot in one of the movies was killed, Larry had said, "If I don't come home, I want to be buried at Arlington."

"I promise," I had assured him, not grasping the uncertainty of making promises during wartime.

We drove to the airport with Laura standing on the front seat between us. The blue metallic upholstery complimented her blue and white gingham dress. Larry looked handsome in his dress blues, his hard-earned silver wings pinned above his pocket. "Blue Eyes Crying in the Rain" played on the radio. I wondered if it was a warning of things to come.

The drive was over too soon. As we pulled into the airport parking lot, I prayed I would do as my mother always said and "act right" so that Larry wouldn't worry. I got out of the passenger seat, gathered Laura in my arms, and walked around to the driver's side, where Larry stood waiting. Perhaps he had rehearsed this scene in his mind, or we were mimicking childhood memories of his own father's good-byes when duty called.

"Don't come inside with me," he directed, as he gathered us in his arms. "You are my beautiful girls." Grinning from ear to ear with the excitement of realizing his lifelong dream of flying planes, he pulled two photos from his wallet. One was of Laura. The other was of me. "These are my two favorite shots of my two favorite girls. They're the ones I'll keep with me always. Honey, I know you'll do this, but be sure to show Laura my picture every day. Tell her, 'This is your Daddy, who loves you very much.'"

He turned to the baby. "Laura, be sweet and do what Mommy asks. Eat good so you'll be strong when Daddy comes home. Daddy loves you."

Sandwiched between the two of us, Laura twisted around to stare at the tears rolling down my face. Larry reached over and wiped them away. "Don't forget, if money gets tight, you have funds in our savings account for emergencies. Everything's going to work out. I have faith in you. It'll be time for R&R before you know it.

"We'll say our good-byes now." He slid Laura to his left hip so that he could kiss me good-bye. His kisses were always sweet and tender, yet strong. This kiss was no different, except it was longer than usual. He pulled me tight to his chest and squeezed. His eyes watered as he traced the outline of my lips with his finger. I stepped back to give him room to be with Laura. He held her out in front of him so they could see into each other's eyes, then pulled her close and kissed her on the cheeks and forehead.

"I love you. Now go to Mommy," he cooed, as he handed her to me. He straightened up tall and erect, as if standing at attention. "Good-bye. I'll always love my girls. Don't look back. The next time you see me, I'll be home."

I didn't watch as Larry turned and walked toward the terminal. In a burst of magical thinking, I hoped that executing his departure just as he'd asked would somehow protect us.

I drove away from the airport, Laura beside me in the front seat. She watched me as she sucked her thumb and hugged her stuffed, yellow lamb to her chest. Our daughter's blond hair, the shape of her face, and her blue eyes resembled her father's so much that at times it was painful for me to look at her. I could still feel Larry's arms around me. I treasured the sensation but grieved what I knew was coming all too soon—the moment when the lingering memory of his touch faded.

I dropped Laura off at the sitter's and headed back to the trailer. Just before he left, Larry had insisted we purchase it so Laura and I would have something of our own if he didn't come home. His acknowledgment of that devastating possibility had made me frantic. To me, the trailer house was a dark omen. It reminded me of the life insurance money my father had purchased. After he died, Mother always said, "It's a good thing your daddy bought that life insurance, or I couldn't have afforded to go back to college." When Larry made plans in the event that he didn't come home, my worst fear felt real, inevitable. Although I didn't agree, Larry purchased the trailer house on credit, along with insurance to pay it off if he didn't return. We'd just spent our last three days together moving into it.

I parked out front and sat in the car, looking at the still unfamiliar house. I'd experienced a lifetime's worth of loss by the time I met Larry. My childhood had been filled with the deaths of several family members, including my father's. I had started drinking at age fourteen to manage my anxiety and quell a lingering sense of dread left in the wake of Daddy's death. I didn't need to drink when Larry and I were together. He told me not to worry, that he loved me and we could do anything we made our minds up to do, and I believed him.

No matter how much I might have wished it, Larry wouldn't be coming home that night. I had learned my childhood lessons well. I could not count on him, no matter how much he promised to always love me. The only person I could count on was myself. Now that Larry was gone, I was Laura's only parent, responsible for paying the bills, going to school, and managing our lives.

This wasn't the first time I had been overwhelmed by a sense of responsibility. Ten weeks earlier, Larry had gone to Fort Walton Beach, Florida, to train on the Cessna O-2. When we married, Larry and I had promised each other that we would love, cherish, and graduate. Larry's dream was to become a pilot in the US Air Force. I planned to be a teacher. We'd decided I should finish the semester at the university in Lubbock, so Laura and I remained in base housing at Reese Air Force Base while Larry trained in Florida. As his deployment to Vietnam drew closer, I had grown more fearful and anxious. Sleepless nights became the norm. When I did manage to sleep, nightmares left me exhausted.

An impending sense of doom took over, as if throughout the time Larry and I had been together, it had been lurking in the shadows, waiting to get me alone. My nose burned like it was on fire, a symptom of anxiety. It began with a tingle and escalated until it throbbed. The greater my fear and worry, the more my nose hurt. I finally confided in a psychiatrist. Alcohol was contraindicated on the bottle of antidepressants he prescribed, so I didn't tell him that I washed them down with a jigger of Jim Beam when I took them. Drinking was my first line of defense to relieve the dread. Binging and purging were also options. But sometimes, even those weren't enough to keep my fears at bay, and I had to take more drastic measures.

After an intense discussion of *Dante's Inferno* in class one day, I couldn't remember where I had parked the car. Like Dante, I couldn't find my way. I walked lost and confused between rows and rows of vehicles in two different university parking lots, anxiety building until I finally found my car. Panicked and hopeless, I sat in the parking lot for over an hour before I was able to drive to the psychiatrist's office. I was in pretty bad shape by the time I reached him. He admitted me to the psychiatric ward at Methodist Hospital for depression and acute anxiety.

Marjorie Lambert, a family friend who babysat Laura while I attended school, offered to keep her while I recuperated. Marjorie's parents, the Scotts, had watched me when I was little. I felt guilty for being gone, but I felt good about leaving Laura with someone I'd known most of my life.

After a few weeks of hospitalization, I returned to classes but spent nights at the hospital. Preoccupied with Larry's upcoming deployment, it was still difficult to concentrate. Time was running out. Finally, my psychiatrist encouraged me to take Laura and go be with Larry in Florida. I could return to school after Larry went to Vietnam. It was all the permission I'd needed to drop out.

Larry rented us a house on the bay side of the Gulf. My fears eased as we built bonfires and boiled shrimp on the beach with the other pilots and their wives. Laura and I built castles in the sand during the day, while Larry trained on the plane he would fly in Vietnam. At night, after Laura was in bed, Larry and I sat on the pier, trailing our feet over the tops of the waves splashing below. As we watched the sun dip below the horizon, he'd slip his arm around my waist and nestle close to me.

"When I'm gone and you're lonely and miss me, look up at the sky and think of me. On the other side of the world, I'll look up at the very same stars and moon and think of you and Laura," he whispered in my ear. The night sky over the water was spectacular. It reminded me of the wide skies of West Texas. But memories of unanswered prayers to those same heavens as a child spoiled my sense of peace.

As I sat in the car outside the trailer, I ached for one more quiet night with Larry like that one, sitting side by side near the water, just being together. My husband was on his way to Vietnam for a whole year. Larry could no longer save me from my desperation. I feared the nightmares would escalate, depression would set in again, and I wouldn't be able to get out of bed.

My nose throbbed. As I grew more and more frantic, I ticked off the tried and true options that brought relief. Binging and purging took too long. Drinking helped, but I didn't want to smell like bourbon when I picked Laura up from the sitter's. I was down to option three.

I got out of the car, hurried into the house, and moved straight to the bathroom. I reached for the "tools" I kept hidden under the sink. Like a surgeon setting out her instruments, I neatly arranged a double-edged razor blade, washcloth, cotton balls, a bottle of rubbing alcohol, and a container of Band-Aids on the bathroom counter. I kneeled down before the toilet, my left arm supported on the seat. I hung my left wrist directly over the toilet bowl. Scared out of my mind, I went to work.

~

TWO

Falling Apart

Despite the cutting I did after Larry left, I kept things somewhat together for about three weeks. I took care of Laura and attended classes, relying on the emotional release of cutting and binging and purging to help me function. Up until Larry's departure, and even on that awful day when he'd left for Nam, I had only made half-hearted scratches on my wrist. I'd never heard about anyone cutting deliberately, but something inside me instinctively believed that if I could bleed out the bad feelings, I might get better. Once Larry was gone, I cut more and more frequently, needing to draw blood. As my emotional state grew more precarious, I stopped preparing for classes. I left Laura at the sitter's for longer periods than my schedule required in case I needed to cut.

I was seeing my psychiatrist once a week but didn't tell him about my secret coping tricks. I was admitted to the psychiatric ward a second time. I'd been there for nearly six weeks when my psychiatrist recommended that I go to the Menninger Clinic in Topeka, Kansas, for treatment. Menninger was one of the best mental hospitals in the country, and the air force would pay for it. My doctor believed I could get well faster with long-term inpatient care. I agreed. I was getting worse, and I was afraid: afraid that I couldn't take care of Laura as she deserved, and afraid for myself.

I felt guilty over not living up to my promises to take care of Laura and stay in school. Paralyzed with shame and disgust, I continued to give in to my feelings and cut or binge and purge.

Sometimes, these behaviors released the pressure of the feelings building inside and gave me the energy to read Laura a story or give her a bath. Other times, cutting or gorging and vomiting were sedatives like drugs or alcohol, and afterward, I slept for hours. I was afraid for Laura to be alone with me. I wasn't afraid of what I might do, I was afraid of what I might forget: forget to feed her, or fall asleep and leave her alone too long.

By the time the psychiatrist suggested inpatient care I was desperate. I would have done anything to get better, but I had to wait for an opening at Menninger. I grew so despondent that I had to go live with my mother in Seminole. I could no longer take care of myself, let alone a toddler. Mother had a full-time teaching job, so Laura stayed in Lubbock with Marjorie and her family.

Being separated from my daughter was even more excruciating than being apart from Larry. I feared that Laura would feel as abandoned as I had when, during my childhood, Mother and Daddy traveled to find heart specialists to help my father. But I had no choice. There were days I couldn't get out of bed except to go to the bathroom.

Mother tried to help me as best she could. In the mornings, she left me in bed while she went to work. When she came home for lunch at noon, I was still there. She coaxed me into getting up and having lunch with her and then went back to work. I stayed in bed most of the day, except for making secret runs to the Dairy Queen to buy mountains of hamburgers, French fries, and ice cream. I consumed the food, purged, and then hid back under the covers. Like cutting, though not as effective, gorging and vomiting relieved my escalating anxiety and the sense that all the fear building up inside of me was about to blow off the top of my head. It kept me going for four weeks, until Menninger finally had a room for me.

In my hometown, everyone knew or wanted to know everyone else's business. I had resented this throughout my childhood and teenage years and often interpreted sincere concern as meddle-some and suffocating. I placed it in the same category as gossip, or worse, intrusion into my family's privacy. Cutting was tough to manage and hard to keep secret. On occasions when I had acciden-tally cut too deep while in Lubbock, I had gone to the emergency room where I'd endured the humiliation of explaining that I had cut myself intentionally. Now that I had moved home to Seminole, I couldn't cut anymore. One trip to the emergency room and the whole town would know I had been there and why.

On the Sunday before I checked into Menninger, Mother and I went to the Baptist church my family had attended since I was two years old. At the end of the service, the minister asked the congre-gation to pray for me. I had asked God many times to help me stop being afraid, to make me able to take care of Laura, and to give me faith that Larry would come home. I prayed the community's prayers would work, since mine hadn't.

After the service, one of the ushers took my elbow and walked me up the aisle. He whispered, "I hope you get well, but I hate to see you go to a psychiatrist. They don't believe in God, you know."

I wrote Larry and told him about my decision to seek inpatient care. In typical Larry style, he wrote back and encouraged me to do what the doctors advised. "I'm hoping you'll get better and be able to join me on R&R," he wrote.

Mother and I boarded a plane, and we were on our way to the Menninger Clinic in Topeka. I was frightened about my decision to institutionalize myself. Was it really the right thing to do? The only knowledge I had of a mental institution was the hospital in Big Springs, down the road from Seminole. Some people in my hometown called it the insane asylum and made jokes about the "inmates" there.

We landed in stormy weather at Kansas City International Airport after dark. We were scheduled to fly on a five-seater to

Topeka, but there was some question as to whether we would be able to take off that evening. I wondered if the thunder clapping and lightening shooting across the sky were an omen of things to come. The wait in the gated area seemed to last forever. Sheets of rain draped a curtain of uncertainty over the windows as I strained to see outside, looking for our plane to arrive.

Finally, the pilot announced the weather had improved enough for us to take off. Mother and I and two other passengers ran across the tarmac and boarded in wet clothes. Once we were in the air, my thoughts shifted to how well I might fit in at the Clinic. While I was at my mother's, I had called a woman my grandmother knew who had been hospitalized at Menninger to ask about the Clinic and the people there. She'd told me that most of the patients were quite wealthy and that it was somewhat like a country club. There was a swimming pool and classes in art, music, and gardening. She'd felt very comfortable there and had gotten better.

I played the piano well but didn't know much about plants. I also worried that I didn't have the right clothes. Our next-door neighbors, Ida Mae and Paul Darling, had taken me shopping when I'd told them I was worried about going to Menninger because I didn't have a wealthy person's wardrobe. Thinking about the navy blue skirt and vest, yellow turtleneck sweater, and dressy slacks in my suitcase made me feel a little more confident.

The next morning, the Clinic sent a cab to the Holiday Inn for Mother and me. We arrived early for my intake appointment, so the cheery receptionist at the admission desk suggested we walk around the grounds. A sidewalk curved throughout the lovely manicured gardens, complete with botanical labels in front of each tree and plant. The old Tudor-style, brick hospital was two stories, with plenty of windows. It reminded me of mansions I had seen in movies. Sidewalks connected the outlying buildings. We passed by small groups or pairs of people, and occasionally just an individual. I didn't see anyone in hospital uniform, so I couldn't tell who worked there and who was a patient. In many ways, it seemed like a college campus, although most of the people were older. I wondered if patients were allowed to go outdoors by themselves.

At the back of the grounds, we came to a greenhouse and a small yard with tree stumps and logs. Two or three men chopped logs while others watched. Mother loved flowers and plants and was intrigued by the greenhouse.

"Look at all these people," she exclaimed. "They aren't lying in bed all day, unable to get up. They're working. I like that. I hope one day you'll get out of bed and get busy, too." She smiled. Neither of us smiled very often these days. I was pleased she felt good about this place but didn't tell her so. I resented the fact that she couldn't understand how I could stay in bed when I had school to finish and a child to care for. I also hoped this was the right place. I had run out of options.

Mother looked down at her watch. "We need to head back. It's almost time."

We had barely sat down in the waiting room when a stout black woman approached us. "Mrs. Hull?" she asked me.

She turned to Mother. "You must be Mrs. Decker. I'm Mrs. Johnson. Please come with me."

As we entered a small conference room with an oval table, a slender, gray-haired man in a gray suit and a tie stood and introduced himself. "Welcome. I'm Doctor Roberts. Won't you have a seat and make yourself comfortable?

"Mrs. Hull, tell me about yourself," Dr. Roberts invited. "How are you feeling?"

I froze. This was real. I was about to check myself into this place, and I had no idea how long I would stay. Should I tell the doctor everything? Even about the cutting and binging and purging? How Daddy had died and left me? How scared I was Larry wouldn't come home from Vietnam? Did I have to tell him about leaving Laura with a sitter? Should I mention how I woke up afraid, how my nose burned continuously, signaling something terrible might happen?

No, I said to myself. *I don't want him to think I'm falling apart.*

Instead I began, "I haven't been doing well. I have trouble getting out of bed, going to school, and not worrying all the time. My psychiatrist in Lubbock said I could get well faster here. That's why I came. I want to get well." Tears spilled from my eyes, betraying my attempts at composure.

Dr. Roberts turned to Mother. "Mrs. Decker, what would you like for me to know about your family and your daughter?"

Mother told him about where we lived, Daddy's heart disease and his death, my older brother and baby sister. She talked about how she'd gone to school to get a college education after Daddy died and my getting in trouble and failing grades in high school. Then she spoke about Larry being in Vietnam and how Laura was staying with a sitter. Mother told Dr. Roberts that I'd been living with her because I was so depressed and stayed in bed every day.

"I was delighted to see the people here up and working in the greenhouse," she added at the end. "Good work is the best cure for a troubled soul."

Dr. Roberts nodded. "Mrs. Johnson, please show Mrs. Hull to her room," he directed.

To me, he said, "Mrs. Johnson will give you a tour of the unit and show you to your room. Your mother and I will continue our visit for a short while. You won't see her again before she leaves, so now is the time to say your good-byes."

A bolt of panic ran through me like the lightening across the sky the night before. I'd had no idea Mother would be leaving so soon. I was going to the ward. I'd be alone in this place. Tears welled in my eyes again.

"Bye, Mom. Tell Laura I love her when you see her next." I hugged her quickly, so she wouldn't see me crying then walked to the door where Mrs. Johnson stood waiting. I didn't look back.

I followed Mrs. Johnson down the green carpet to a set of double doors. As she reached for the keys dangling from her wrist to unlock them, a voice inside my head screamed, *What have you done, you idiot? You just walked onto a locked ward. You must be crazy. You deserve to be here.* My nose throbbed as the lock clicked shut behind us.

~~~

THREE

Deployed to Menninger

Mrs. Johnson and I passed a nurse in starched white hospital regalia seated in the hallway. She seemed to be guarding the elevator and a door that opened onto the circle drive outside. We walked down a hall, past patient rooms on both sides. Mrs. Johnson stopped about two-thirds of the way down.

"It's small but adequate." She unlocked the door. "It'll seem more like home once you put your own things out. You've got a half bath, closet, dresser, desk, and a twin bed, just like in a dorm room." She told me my luggage would be delivered, and we'd go through it together.

I must have looked surprised. "Sharps," she explained. "Anything sharp, like scissors, fingernail clippers, razor blades, anything that could be used to hurt yourself or someone else, must be kept under lock in the nurses' station.

"Make yourself comfortable and come on down to the nurses' station at the end of the hall when you're ready. I'll give you a tour of the unit."

Mrs. Johnson left. I sat down on the bed. I heard Larry's voice: "Tyra, you can do this. Do what the doctors tell you and the three of us will be together again before you know it. Do good. Do your best. I love you."

I grasped onto a memory that sustained me: Larry, Laura, and me back in Ft. Walton Beach, the three of us playing in the sand by the water. I prayed that if things went well and I did my best, God would let me meet Larry for R&R in Hawaii. My daydream turned to a real dream as I laid my head down on the pillow and slept.

Startled and disoriented, I awoke two hours later in the strange room still devoid of any of my personal belongings. Craving a cup of coffee and a cigarette, I dressed and headed down the hall. An aide supervised me while I smoked outside the nurses' station. She informed me that Mrs. Johnson was in conference with the evening staff, who were just coming on duty. I decided to go down to the patient lounge.

The large room was furnished with several sofas and chairs and small tables. Board games were stacked neatly on a corner table. One card table held loose puzzle pieces and a box with a picture of what the completed puzzle should look like.

A small hi-fi record player and a piano assured me I wouldn't have to be without my most acceptable coping tool: music. I'd taken piano lessons at age seven when Daddy, a car dealer, had traded a used car for a piano. When the piano was delivered, I'd promised him I'd learn to play beautifully. I took lessons for nine years and loved it. It helped me feel close to Daddy after he died.

The small kitchenette included a hot plate and pot of water for making tea and coffee, Styrofoam cups, and stirrers. Beneath the counter, a small refrigerator sat next to wooden cartons of soda. One carton held the empties. I sat down at the card table and made a half-hearted effort to add a piece to the small bunch of puzzle pieces someone had already put together. I hadn't worked on a puzzle since I was little.

A large shadow fell over the puzzle. I looked up. The woman towering over me scared the shit out of me. She stood about 5'11". She rocked back and forth next to the card table. A wad of blue yarn dangled from knitting needles she held in her outstretched arms.

"Who are you?" she asked, staring straight ahead, trancelike.

Rather than wait for my response, she robotically turned her clogs toward the door and shuffled into the hallway.

As the daunting woman left, a young kid with greasy hair growing over his ears and down the back of his neck flopped down in a chair across from me. He wore a filthy white T-shirt and jeans. "That's Emily," he said, as the woman shuffled out. "You're new. Why are you here? Did someone make you come? What's your story?

"I'm George," he blurted before I could answer his questions. "Hey, do you play the piano? I sing, but no one here will play for me. Do you play?"

"A little," I replied. "Maybe sometime we'll play and sing. Depends on what kind of music they have. I don't know any sing-along music by heart." I was talking almost as fast as he was.

"That's okay," he said. "The food's really great here once you get to go downstairs to the cafeteria. But you aren't going anywhere until they give you all your psychological tests, and they know what kind of nutty you are. You'll have to eat on trays for two weeks, until they finish. They don't ask you what you want to eat when you're on trays; they decide for you.

"Anyway, if you need anything, you just come to me, and I'll show you the ropes. Anything you want to know right now? Ever been hospitalized before? What did you say your diagnosis was? Okay, gotta go. See you later!"

George left, and I jumped when I noticed a beautiful, tall, slender brunette sitting in a corner of the room reading a book. I hadn't seen her earlier. She looked over at me.

"Hi, I'm Lainey. Where are you from? When did you get here?" Though dressed in denim jeans and a sweater, her stately demeanor telegraphed money. I was relieved I had worn my new, blue knit skirt and matching vest with the yellow turtleneck sweater.

"I'm Tyra. I just got here today. I'm from West Texas," I answered. "Where're you from?"

"Oh, that's great," she exclaimed. "I'm from New Mexico, right next door. What does your husband do?"

"His name's Larry, and he's a pilot in the air force. He's in Vietnam. We have a little girl who's almost two years old. She's with her babysitter while I'm here," I offered.

"Really?" She leaned forward. "My first husband was a pilot in the air force, too. But he died. I remarried. The new one's a scoundrel," she added matter-of-factly.

My nose burned as I imagined Larry's plane crashing.

"Our governess stays with my two—a boy and a girl. Thank God they don't have to leave home while I'm here. She's going to bring them for a visit when my doctor gives his approval.

"This place is all right," she added. "Except the shopping is terrible. They say they don't take anyone here as a patient unless they think they can get well. Remember that." She arched an eyebrow and looked doubtful. "There's one lady who's been here over seven years, though.

"There are some things that are important and make you feel more normal," she continued, "like shopping at White Lakes Mall. After you've been here a while, perhaps you can get permission to go the mall in the Menninger van, with supervision of course." She sighed. "They never give me a large enough allowance. But it doesn't matter, since there's no Neiman's or any other elegant stores here."

Mrs. Johnson stuck her head into the lounge. "Mrs. Hull, your luggage is here. Let me introduce you to Mrs. Locke. She's an aide on the evening shift. She'll sit with you in your room as you go through the contents of your luggage. You'll start to feel at home once you have all your belongings put away."

FOUR

Meeting Larry

Short and stocky, Mrs. Locke wore glasses and a mischievous smile. "We're going to get on well," she said as she extended her right hand forward to shake mine. As we walked down the hall to my room, I couldn't take my eyes off Mrs. Locke's red hair. She wasn't pretty, but her energy was warm and comforting.

I felt apprehensive unpacking my bags while someone I didn't know watched. It wasn't that I was hiding anything; it just felt intrusive and rude. It made me feel like an inmate. *How did you think it would be in a mental hospital?* I chastised myself.

"Let's put your suitcase on the bed. You sit next to it." Mrs. Locke pulled a chair closer to the twin bed.

"I'll sit here and make a record of any sharps: scissors, nail clippers, anything that could be dangerous. Any time you want an item, just come and ask a nurse or an aide for it. They'll check it out to you and stay with you while you use it, then they'll mark it returned when you're finished. I'll also list everything in your luggage, so if there's ever a mix-up in the laundry room or something of yours gets lost, we'll have a record of what belongs to you," she explained.

It sounded like a prison. I resented it. If I had the gumption to check myself into a mental hospital, surely I deserved to be trusted. Then again, I was cutting and binging and purging. And I had pretended at my intake meeting with Dr. Roberts that I felt better than I really did. Why should anyone trust me?

"Do you have any questions?" Mrs. Locke asked.

Shaking my head, I removed a notebook from my suitcase. Mrs. Locke listed it on a numbered sheet of paper. "I understand your husband's in Vietnam, and you have a little girl." Mrs. Locke smiled. "Is that right?"

"Yes ma'am." I pulled a double picture frame holding two five-by seven-inch photos from my suitcase. "Here they are. This is Laura," I pointed to the photo of Laura laughing, her chubby little hands clapping. "And this is my Larry. He looks so proud in his dress blues." Tears rolled down my cheeks in spite of my efforts to choke them back.

"I know this must be hard," Mrs. Locke spoke softly. "The good news is you have all the support you need here, and you have one of the best doctors at the Clinic. Laura is with good people, or you wouldn't have left her with them. And Mrs. Hull, I'll keep Larry in my thoughts."

I managed a weak smile. "When I'm not so tired, I'll tell you about Larry and Laura. I miss them desperately."

"I'd like to hear all about them, whenever you feel like telling me. Take a few minutes for yourself now. I'll let you know when your tray is here." She gently closed the door as she left.

Grateful for the privacy, I laid my head down on the pillow and sobbed. Mother had already left me at Menninger and was headed home to Texas. A familiar knot of worry tightened in my stomach. I was reminded of the time when I was ten years old and babysat my sister, Susannah. It was her first birthday, and a young college couple that lived nearby was having a party for her. Before Mother left for afternoon classes, she'd told me to dress the baby in her new pink Sunday outfit by 4:30 that afternoon, since she'd barely have time to pick us up after class and get to the party.

Susannah and I were dressed on time and waiting. Mother had said she'd be home about 5:00, after her class was over. From the screened-in porch of our second-floor apartment, I watched for her car to turn the corner onto our street. The minute hand moved past 5:00. The baby grew fussy. The longer we waited, the bigger the knot in my stomach got. After Daddy died, I worried about losing Mother. She was all we had.

Five-thirty came and went. Fighting back panic, I straddled the baby on my hip and walked down the staircase, around the street corner, and up the hill toward the university. My heart leaped as a car the same color of our Chevrolet came down the hill toward us.

As the station wagon slowed to a stop, I saw Mother at the wheel. Clinging tight to my sister, I ran as best I could to the car. "Mother, I was so worried about you," I called through the open window. Tears streamed down my cheeks. "I was so scared you weren't coming back."

Mother was furious. "What are you doing out here?" she admonished. "I told you to wait at home. We got out of class late. When I'm late, you're to stay where I left you. Something could have happened to you." She got out of the car, took Susannah, and said, "Hurry. We're going to be late." I was heartbroken. I wanted to make her proud. I did my best to take care of our baby.

Now, Mother was on a plane back to Texas, and Laura was with a friend, not family. I was alone in a mental institution in Kansas, and Larry was in Vietnam fighting a war. *Are we all ever going to be together again? Does Laura feel lost and alone, like I did when my parents left? What have I done? What have I done to Laura?* I wondered.

That first evening at Menninger, I wanted to call my mother and have her come pick me up, but this was one time I couldn't go home just because I was homesick and afraid. I wasn't a child anymore. I had to straighten up and act right, like Mother always said. Larry was at war, my baby was miles away in Texas, and I had admitted myself to a mental hospital. I needed to be a grown up and get well. Larry's voice whispered in my head, just like on the cassette tapes he'd sent me: "Do what the doctors tell you, girl, so you can meet me for R&R. Remember, I love you."

With his encouragement, I walked down the hall to the food cart for my tray.

A couple of patients were having dinner together at a small table. I considered joining them but instead took my tray back to my room. Being alone with a whole tray of food was unnerving. I feared that if I ate it, especially the pumpkin pie, I'd trigger a binge, but I had no more pie and nowhere to go to satisfy the compulsion. I moved the food around on my plate then dumped half of it in the toilet and walked my tray down to the cart parked outside the nurses' station. Mrs. Locke wasn't anywhere in sight. I headed back to my room. She had said there was bed check every night, so I shouldn't be concerned if I heard my door open and close.

The day had seemed to last forever. I didn't want to be awake at bed check, and I didn't want to talk with anyone else. I put on my pajamas, knelt by the bed, and whispered the same prayer I said every night: "God, please watch over Laura and please don't let her think I wanted to leave her. Please protect Larry. Please help me to get well. God, please help us."

I crawled into bed and thought about Larry, my beautiful blond-haired husband who loved me no matter what. I closed my eyes and escaped back into one of the brightest times in my life, our first date.

~~~

The first thing that had crossed my mind when Larry picked me up in his '57 Chevy was that Daddy would have approved. My father had been manager and junior partner of the Chevrolet dealership in Seminole, Texas. He'd always said you could tell a lot about a man's character by the way he kept his car. The chrome on Larry's two-toned lavender and white '57 Chevy Bel Air sparkled; the shimmery black interior was immaculate. The way Larry treated his car reminded me of my father, who'd taken pride in his automobiles and driven them with confidence and grace. Daddy had lived his life the same way, confident and proud.

"We're going to Reese to watch the planes land and take off," Larry explained, as we drove off that late September day in 1965. "Is that okay with you? I never get tired of watching the same landing patterns over and over. I'm going to officer training school after I graduate and after that, to pilot training."

On the way to the base, Larry told me about his family. His dad, Robert J. Hull, was a chief master sergeant in the air force. The base in Roswell, New Mexico, was home. Larry's mother and younger brother were living there while his dad was on temporary duty in Thailand. Larry's life sounded so different from mine. I was third-generation Texas on both sides. Both sets of my grandparents were farmers, and most of my relatives lived within a hundred-mile radius of my hometown, Seminole.

"Sounds like my mom's family in Alabama," Larry said when I told him about my relatives. "My grandparents are country people, too. But I've grown up an air force brat and loved it. I'm going to be an officer and a pilot after I graduate," he declared proudly. A college sophomore with an engaging crooked grin, Larry Hull projected a wholesome, boy-next-door image. Even so, he spoke with such intensity and conviction that I believed he would become anything he wanted.

"How long have you wanted to be a pilot?" I quizzed him.

"Since I was seven. Dad was stationed in Japan. We lived on the base, and I attended school there. We practiced getting under the desks during air raid drills." Larry shot me a grin.

"I knew one day I'd fly planes. My family will live on the officers' side of the base."

"What's different about living on the officers' side?" I knew nothing about military bases.

"Only officers are pilots. That's the main thing," Larry explained.

"Everything is based on rank in the military. Base housing is divided into sections. Officers and their families live in one section. There's another section for noncommissioned officers, because their rank is different. My best friends' dads were officers. Officers have their own club, and housing is nicer on their side. I want that for my family and me."

"Isn't it hard on your mom, with your dad gone so much?" We passed the main gate to Reese Air Force Base. Larry pulled off the highway and parked where the road paralleled the runway. He turned off the ignition and rolled down his window.

"It's his job." He shrugged. "Men like my dad keep the air force flying. Without them, planes would be grounded.

"What does your dad do?" he asked, looking over at me.

"He died when I was nine," I told Larry. "He was sick for two years. The doctors said he had hardening of the arteries. A heart attack killed him, but it wasn't his first. He grew up on a farm eating fried eggs and ham and biscuits and gravy. His cholesterol was off the charts. From when I was seven until he died, it seemed like he and Mom were gone most of the time, looking for a doctor that could help him.

"My parents were happy before Daddy got sick," I recalled. "Mother and Daddy always said that Daddy brought home the bacon and Mother cooked it. They were crazy about each other. 'I've had my eye on your daddy since I was in third grade,' Momma liked to brag.

"Daddy wore white, starched shirts with a suit and tie on workdays. On the weekend, he would roll up his sleeves and put on a pair of slacks. Mother took great pride in ironing his shirts, making sure he had a fresh one every single day."

Memories flashed in my mind as I told Larry about my parents and how I'd stayed with either my aunt and uncle or friends while they sought someone who could save my father's life. I'd felt so lost when my parents left on those trips, so afraid they wouldn't come back for my brother and me. Daddy's heart trouble and my parents' absences changed me. I became sad and afraid.

"I idolized my daddy." I choked back tears. I didn't want to cry in front of this boy I barely knew. But Larry Hull was so easy to talk to. It felt as if we'd known each other a long time.

"It hasn't been the same since Daddy died," I admitted, tears springing despite my resolve.

"How awful!" Larry's grin evaporated. "How old was he?" he asked.

"Only thirty-six when he died. Mom was thirty-four, my brother was thirteen, and I was nine. My baby sister was born three months after Daddy died." Nine years had passed, yet my voice still broke whenever I spoke about losing my father.

Larry stretched an arm around my shoulders, comforting me. "How did y'all get by after that?"

"Mother sold Daddy's share of the Chevrolet dealership. The money from the sale, coupled with Daddy's life insurance and social security benefits, was almost enough for us to live on while Mother went back to complete the three years of college she had left after she'd dropped out and married Daddy. We left Seminole during the summers for Mother to go to college in Alpine, near Big Bend National Park. It was only four hours away from our hometown, but it felt like a whole different world," I explained.

Larry nodded. "If my dad hadn't married Mom and adopted me when I was three and taken us out of the hills of Alabama, I would have ended up working in the lumber mills or oil rigs off the Gulf Coast. I probably wouldn't have gone to college. Their marriage gave us a life of travel and new experiences."

"Yes, good things happened for us, too, when Mother went to college at Sul Ross," I said. "On weekends, we went rock hunting in the mountains with her classmates and their children, and I got to see *The Glass Menagerie* on the big stage at the college. It was magical. During Mom's senior year we moved to Alpine so she could complete her student teaching requirement.

"After she graduated, we moved back to Seminole, where Mother was hired to teach third grade. She built the new house she and Daddy had always wanted. It sounds awful, but in some ways our life got better after Daddy died." I felt guilty admitting how much I had loved Alpine, our new house, and enjoying a new status in our hometown once Mother became a teacher.

Moving back and forth between Seminole and Alpine had been fun but challenging. As I thought about Larry's life on military bases, I wondered out loud what it would be like to live somewhere like Washington, DC, or even overseas.

"The air force is a way to have a good life and travel. For example, you can go anywhere in the world and be a teacher or a principal," Larry winked, referring to what I'd told him earlier about my plans to become a teacher like my mother. "There are schools on air force bases all over the world." His eyes sparkled with barely concealed meaning.

I hardly knew Larry Hull, but I got the sense he was trying to talk me into coming along on his adventures. The thought made me giddy. Larry was exciting, so full of potential it buzzed in the air around him. He pointed to the plane above our heads, which was on final approach for landing. Its engines roared as it passed through the West Texas clouds just above the horizon, as if strung from the heavens by an invisible cable.

"That's gonna be me in the cockpit someday," he declared with such confidence I had no doubt he was right. I had dreams, too.

Before that day, I had never met anyone as determined as I was to accomplish them. In Larry Hull, I had met my match.

A short time later, Larry slid his car into the parking lot of a strip mall in front of a restaurant called "Pop's." I was struck by how quickly he appeared at my door once he turned off the ignition. We stepped inside the tiny cafe, where an elderly gentleman wearing a white paper chef's hat trimmed in red greeted us.

"So you're having supper with me," Pop ribbed Larry. "Who's your friend?"

Larry grinned. "Someone you're going to like, Pop."

We sat down at a Formica table, and Pop served up two teeming plates of spaghetti. As we ate, we continued to share childhood stories. I wanted Larry to appreciate how close I had been to my father, how much I had lost when Daddy died.

"When Daddy got sicker, sometimes he stayed home to rest instead of going to church on Sunday mornings. My favorite times were when I got to stay home and be with him. I was seven or eight years old," I began. "We had a private joke. It was a story I made up about how old people get to heaven.

"The preacher stood in the pulpit, his red mad face yelling about going to hell when you died. With sweat pouring down his face, he'd scream, 'If you aren't saved, you'll burn in hell. Sinners burn in the dark pit of fire and brimstone, gnashing their teeth forever.'

"'Daddy,' I'd say to my father, 'we don't need to worry about old Mr. and Mrs. Garfield. They're going to heaven! Know how I know, Daddy? Cause they already lost their teeth. No teeth, Daddy. Get it?'

"Then I'd yell out the punch line, 'Old people trade their teeth in for a ticket to heaven!'

"Daddy and I competed to see which one of us could laugh the loudest, forcing tears through our squinted eyes each time I told the story. It was our ritual," I told Larry.

Although he laughed at the punch line, Larry immediately grew somber. "Losing him was like losing your best friend, wasn't it?"

We continued sharing stories over dessert. Larry told me about living with his grandparents outside Mobile, Alabama. Picking wild grapes and chasing butterflies on the mountain when he was a little boy was never far from his mind. We talked for hours. It was as if we needed to catch each other up on all the years that had passed before we'd met.

Soon Pop was back at our table whispering softly, "Hey guys, I got to close."

I felt such a strong connection with this beautiful blue-eyed boy. I had felt it that afternoon at the runway, and it grew stronger as we talked at Pop's. As I marveled at the magic happening between us, a silent voice within me said, *I know you. I know what it's like to have a dream.*

When Larry dropped me off at home that night, the stars shone especially bright across the velvety West Texas sky. Larry escorted me to my front porch, his arm looped through mine. Squeezing my hand at the door, his intense blue eyes locked with mine. "May I call you tomorrow?" he asked.

~

FIVE

Nitroglycerin

I awoke at Menninger the next morning feeling disoriented. I wanted to be back with Larry. I closed my eyes, hoping I would wake up in that other, brighter reality of when we'd first met. But it didn't work. I was in a mental hospital. No wishing or praying was going to change that. I had no idea what time it was. I dreaded walking down the hall to the women's shower room and instead turned over and tried to go back to sleep.

I was supposed to have psychological tests over the next two weeks, but no one had told me when I would start them. After a little while, a staff person stuck her head in and announced my tray had arrived and was on the cart next to the nurses' station. I told her I didn't want breakfast.

"Maybe you'll change your mind, but don't wait too long," she cautioned. "The dining room staff is punctual about picking up the trays."

Growing more and more anxious the longer I sat alone in my room, I pulled on some slacks, a top, and a pair of slippers. I ran my fingers through my hair and wandered down the hall to the nurses' station. The halls were empty, although I noted another patient peering from behind her door. *She looks worse than me*, I thought. I wondered whether I could get that bad.

A nurse stepped out of the office. "Good morning," she said. "Sleep well?"

I nodded, the voice in my head taunting me. *Liar, liar. There you go again.* The large round clock on the wall inside the nurses' station said 10:00 a.m.

"Do you know what my schedule is for my psychological tests?" I asked. "When the first one is?"

"I'm not sure we've received your orders yet. Let me look." The nurse thumbed through some papers on the desk. "I don't see them. We'll let you know. I expect it'll be tomorrow but Dr. Roberts left a message that he'll see you today about 3:00."

Around noon, I walked down the hall and sat in a chair in the hallway outside the nurses' station. Soon, the dining staff appeared with the lunch cart. I took a tray and went back to my room. My mind raced with memories of Larry, Laura, and my mother and disbelief that my life had come to this. My anxiety raged without my tried and true antidotes of cutting and gorging and purging. I wondered why I'd thought checking myself into the Clinic was the answer. *What were you thinking? You must be crazy!* My brain throbbed as I lashed out at myself.

The food on my tray looked all right, but I couldn't eat. *Ironic,* I thought, *if I can't eat and purge, I don't want to put anything in my mouth.* I felt trapped. I made myself eat a bite, flushed the rest down the toilet, and walked my tray down to the food cart. I glanced at the clock in the nurses' station: only 12:30. I still had two and a half hours before Dr. Roberts came.

Back in my room, I sat on the bed and pulled out a letter I'd received from Larry before I came to Menninger. I hung on every one of his encouraging words: "I love you. Do good. Get well and do what the doctors tell you. Do it for Laura and do it for me. I believe in you." I lay down and waited.

Finally, there was a knock on the door. "Mrs. Hull," Dr. Roberts said as he entered, "how are you today?"

"Tolerable," I said.

He smiled. "I haven't heard that response in a long time."

"I'm trying to be positive," I said.

"Tell me about your day."

Tears fell as I told him how lost I felt, how I wondered if I should have come, how I missed and worried about Larry and Laura.

"Why did you come?" he asked.

"Because my psychiatrist said I could get better faster here," I sniffled.

"What do you think?" he asked.

"I wasn't getting better at home, and I want to get better but, Dr. Roberts, today has been awful. I'm homesick, and I don't feel like I belong here. But I feel that way no matter where I am," I whined.

"It'll get better," he assured me. "Tomorrow morning, one of the staff members will walk you over to the psychologist's office for your first test. Your tests will help us understand more about how you're feeling. They will help us help you. Many people find them interesting, and some even enjoy them.

"You'll want to eat breakfast before you go for your first test tomorrow. I believe your appointment is at 10:00." He looked down at a folder with some papers in it. "The following day, you have an appointment with the medical doctor for a physical and later on, at the end of the week or the next, a dental appointment. All our patients have these exams and tests. We want to know how you are doing physically as well as psychologically, since physical health affects psychological health," he explained.

"I'll see you tomorrow around 3:00 again. I understand you enjoy coffee. Perhaps we'll walk down to the dining room and get a cup there. Would you like that?"

I nodded.

"I'll see you tomorrow, then. Remember to eat tonight and breakfast tomorrow." He smiled as he got up from his chair and left.

I felt better. There was something about Dr. Roberts that made me feel safe. His eyes were kind, like my grandfather, PaPa's. He also seemed professional. Dr. Roberts would help me get well. *Thank God*, I thought, *thank God I've found someone to help.*

The next afternoon, Dr. Roberts asked me how the tests had gone that morning. In one of them, the psychologist had shown me a picture of a little boy asleep in his bed. A man wearing a bandana and carrying a revolver was climbing in the boy's bedroom window. I knew this meant trouble for the little boy, but instead of telling the psychologist what I saw, I'd told him that the picture depicted a little boy sleeping. His father was climbing in the window because he'd locked himself out. The gun was for taking the boy hunting. I was afraid to tell the psychologist my true interpretation of the photo because I feared there was something wrong with me.

Now I admitted to Dr. Roberts what I'd really seen when I looked at the picture. It felt similar to what I had done when I first met him the day I was admitted. I was miserable and afraid of losing Larry and of being away from Laura, but I had diminished how bad I felt. "Why didn't I tell you how I really felt? Why didn't I tell the psychologist what I really saw? There's something wrong with me," I announced. "What is it?"

"We'll work together to find answers to those questions," Dr. Roberts assured me. "But first, your mother talked about your father's illness and fatal heart attack at your intake meeting. What can you tell me about that time?"

"Well, I was just seven years old when I found out about it," I said. "Daddy and I were close. When our family played Parcheesi and other games, we were always partners, and Mother and my brother, Rodney, were on the same team," I explained.

"Daddy didn't always go to church. Sometimes, I got to stay home with him rather than go with Mother and Rodney. One Sunday something pretty awful happened," I told Dr. Roberts slowly.

Memories of my father's illness came rushing back, as if it had been yesterday instead of almost sixteen years ago. "Daddy read the *Lubbock Avalanche Journal* while I cozied up against him and fell asleep under the bedspread, because there was freezing air blowing from the swamp cooler in my parents' bedroom."

I glanced at Dr. Roberts to see if it was okay to continue. He looked at me intently, listening. "I awoke to Daddy gasping for air," I went on.

"I turned over just in time to see him reaching for the small bottle of tiny white pills on the nightstand next to the bed. His face was pale, his lips bluish-purple. I couldn't understand what he was trying to tell me, he was gasping so hard. He pointed to the pill bottle on the nightstand. I crawled over him, crying and apologizing for pushing my knee into his stomach in my desperation to grab his pills."

I closed my eyes for a moment as the memory of that awful day overwhelmed me. I could see it all again so clearly, even though it had happened so long ago. "The bottle fell onto the floor and rolled under the bed," I told Dr. Roberts.

"I tried to catch it, but instead I fell off the bed.

"Dr. Roberts, I realized this might just be it. Daddy could die, and it would be my fault." I stopped.

"Go on if you can," Dr. Roberts encouraged.

"I inched my way underneath the bed frame, grappling in the darkness for the tiny bottle. I lunged for it too hard and pushed those precious pills farther beneath the bed. I tried to hold my breath, so I could hear whether or not Daddy was still breathing. Then I slammed my forehead into one of the bed slats. The pill bottle was wedged against a pillow under the bed, but I was able to wrap my fingers around it and back out quickly. I was scared to death to stand up, afraid of what I'd see, that maybe Daddy had . . .

"I got off the floor with one hand wrapped around the medicine bottle. I grabbed the mattress with the other hand and used it to steady myself. I saw Daddy's head resting on his pillow, his face ashen, his lips blue. I frantically unscrewed the cap then dropped the first pill but grabbed another one just before the rest of them spilled to the floor. I opened Daddy's mouth with one hand and pushed the pill under his tongue, just like I had seen him do." I paused again, out of breath. I had been racing to tell the story, just like I'd raced to get my father his precious medicine.

"It took forever before Daddy's eyelids fluttered," I recalled. "His chest barely moved, but thank God he was breathing and had quit gasping.

"The front door opened and Mother yelled, 'Anybody home?' As she walked into the bedroom, I told her I didn't think Daddy was feeling so good. She sat down on the bed next to Daddy, and I went to the bathroom and vomited my Sunday lunch.

"Dr. Roberts, I didn't tell my mother that Daddy needed his nitroglycerin pills and couldn't get them himself because he felt so bad. I didn't tell her how I had to get them and that they fell on the floor and I was scared. Why couldn't I say that?

"The same thing happened the day the psychologist asked me to tell him what I saw in pictures," I explained. "I couldn't say the words when I saw the man coming in through the window even though I thought something terrible was about to happen to that little boy. Why didn't I tell the truth about what I really saw? What's wrong with me?"

SIX

A New Class Schedule

Unlike most of the Menninger house doctors, Dr. Roberts was special because he usually stopped by on Saturday mornings. The weekend after I finished my tests, he announced I was officially on group status, which meant I could go on walks with other patients supervised by a staffer, eat meals in the dining room, take classes, and go to the canteen for toiletries, sundries, snacks, and paperback books.

Dr. Roberts and I discussed which classes I could take in the educational center. He suggested sewing, art, and gym.

"I really don't like handmade clothes," I told him when he mentioned sewing. "Mother made most of my clothes, and I always felt everyone knew it. After Daddy died, we didn't have much money. When I was in sixth grade, Mother had just enough for material for three sets of matching skirts and blouses. One of my friends in band practice teased me for always wearing the same three outfits."

"Mrs. Hull, I hear you, but I'd like you to try sewing," Dr. Roberts urged. "Mona is a good instructor. Staying busy when you're not feeling well can be beneficial.

"You mentioned band in sixth grade. What instrument did you play?"

"The flute. But my favorite instrument is the piano."

"I'll see if that can be arranged." Dr. Roberts took my suggestions seriously and treated me like I was worthy of being heard. During my past hospitalizations in Lubbock, I had felt talked down to, but at Menninger, I felt like I had some say in my treatment. It gave me hope.

"Now, how about gym?" Dr. Roberts asked.

"I don't like sports," I whined. "I'm not good at them. I don't enjoy physical activity."

"Why is that?"

"I used to get terrible asthma attacks playing kick the can in the neighborhood. I had to use an inhaler. I couldn't breathe in gym class. I don't have good experience with physical activity," I summarized.

"After Daddy died, my brother teased me mercilessly about being fat. 'You look like a bowling ball with hair,' he'd say. I had a round face and begged Mother to cut my long curls. But Rodney was right. I did look like a bowling ball with hair," I reported.

"Between asthma and feeling fat and clumsy, I'm self-conscious. I've avoided physical activity at all costs. When my friends in high school went out for sports, I tried out to be the manager, so I could go on team trips and be involved but not have to play."

"I recommend and want you to be in gym class," Dr. Roberts said. "Kyle is the leader. In spite of your reluctance, perhaps this will be a good experience for you. I also want you to go on group walks whenever possible."

I nodded, willing to give it a try. "What about an art class?" I asked. "I'd like to try pottery or sculpting. One of the patients brought a dove he'd made out of clay back to the patient lounge. Maybe I could make one of those."

"That's a pretty full schedule if you include art."

"You're right," I agreed. "I should see how things go." I hesitated a moment then added, "Dr. Roberts, what did my tests tell you about how I'm doing? Do you think I can get well?"

"I do," he said. "You're sad, and you have reason to be. You miss Larry and Laura, and you're concerned about them. And you still miss your father. We believe you'll feel better when you're busier and when you spend more time with people. You're smart, and you don't have to do this alone.

"How do you think you're doing?" he asked. "How are you feeling?"

"Tolerable." I answered the same way I had last time.

~~~~~~

SEVEN

Group Walk to the Pond

After lunch, my last meal on trays in my room, I wandered down to the lounge. Because it was a Saturday and no classes were scheduled, more patients than usual were gathered there. I sprawled out on the floor next to the piano and arranged several pairs of shoes and polishing paraphernalia around me. Being with people made me feel less lonely.

George, the young man with the dirty T-shirt I'd met my first day on the unit, was stretched out on the long sofa. "Want to play the piano while I sing?" he asked in a begging kind of way. He reminded me of a stray puppy.

"Not today," I replied. I stared down at the scuffed loafers in my hand. *How am I going to make these look newer*, I wondered?

"Okay then, when?" he pressed.

"When I feel like I it," I snapped. I kept my eyes on my shoes.

He seemed to accept my answer, but I had a strong feeling it was only for the time being.

Emily shuffled into the lounge and parked her full height before me. She stared down at me. No words, just staring. I continued to work the burgundy polish into the cracked leather.

From across the room, a woman about my age smiled at me. I had met Deborah in the hall one day. She was single and from Iowa. "How's it going?" she asked. "On group yet?"

"Yes, as of today. I can go on the group walk this afternoon and down to the dining room for dinner tonight." I was surprised

at the pride in my voice. *Guess it's the little things that count here,*
I thought.

A gray-haired man was sitting alone at a small table in front of
a plastic chess set. All the pieces were set up, ready to play. As I
polished, I eyed him out of the corner of my eye and caught him
doing the same back. I laid my loafers down on a towel and walked
over to his table.

"Hi, I'm Tyra. Do you play?"

"Yes, I do, but I usually can't find a partner. I'm The Minister."
He extended his right hand.

As we shook hands, he asked, "How about a game?"

"Not now. I have group privileges as of today, and I'm looking
forward to a walk this afternoon before dinner. Then I'm going to
the dining room." I proudly explained my status to him just as I
had to Deborah.

Why am I explaining this to everyone? I wondered. *Because what
you are allowed to do reflects how you're doing,* I reminded myself.
*Wherever you are, people want to know where you fit in. That's how
they know how to treat you.*

My sophomore year in high school I'd been allowed to drive
Mother's car to the Dairy Queen for lunch. Freedom to come and
go had been huge as a teenager. Now, I had to earn it all over again.

"How about tomorrow?" I asked him.

"Four o'clock?" he shot back.

I nodded. "Here, at this table?"

A thin smile crossed his lips.

I had just lined up a date to play chess at the mental institution with a real minister. I bet he believed in God. A real minister
had checked himself into this place, seeking help. Wouldn't the
usher at Seminole First Baptist Church back home be surprised? I
wasn't the only one who needed more help than what the church

people and their prayers could provide. If God's chosen could be afflicted, it was possible my sickness was not a punishment for being such a wretched sinner. This brought me some comfort. But since I relied on God's power and strength to protect Larry and to cure me, it was also horrific. God hadn't even protected The Minister, a loyal servant.

Mrs. Locke stepped into the lounge just as I was gathering up my shoes and polish. She motioned for me to join her as she announced, "All those on group who are ready for a walk, we'll be leaving in a few minutes. Get your coats. It's brisk out this afternoon."

I carried my things back to my room then met the group at the nurses' station. An aristocratic-looking man named Forbes, George, Lainey, and I all lined up.

Mrs. Locke checked off our names with the head nurse and unlocked the outside door. We all stepped out. Being outdoors felt new and fresh. My nose wasn't burning. I was the last one out and followed a few steps behind the group. Even though winter was coming on, the grounds were beautiful, not brown and dry like West Texas. The crisp October air felt good on my cheeks.

The manicured grounds at Menninger reminded me of Larry. Somehow, everything reminded me of him. I noticed several pairs of empty chairs along the path as we walked from the main building where we lived toward the pond at one corner of the campus. Always two chairs, never just one. You didn't have to be alone here. There were people to talk with. Larry would appreciate that. He would approve of this place, with its manicured grounds and beautiful landscape. I made a mental note to describe them to him in my next letter. I wondered if his room in Vietnam was as small as mine at the Clinic and what the pilots in his unit were like. In a strange way I realized our lives were similar, which brought some comfort. We were both away from home, both of us were separated from Laura and each other, and we both depended on strangers for our very lives—Larry on his comrades and commanding officers, me on the doctors and Clinic staff.

Larry faced enemy fire and death every day. I was my own worst enemy, cruel at times, fearful for my sanity, and alone in a strange place. Laura and Larry needed me to get well so our family could be together. Larry would do his best to come home. I was committed to doing my part, too. My fight was different from his war; nonetheless, it was the fight of my life.

Thick, tall trees and privacy hedges lined the campus perimeter, buffering the Clinic grounds from the adjacent streets. I could hear the traffic on Gage Boulevard. We followed the dirt path down a slope toward one corner of the campus. The path led to a small pond with a tiny wooden bridge, surrounded by mature trees and bushes. The area reminded me of Lackland Air Force Base in San Antonio, where Larry had attended Officer Training School before pilot training. I'd been pregnant with Laura that Christmas. We'd spent a good part of Larry's twenty-four-hour pass downtown at the River Walk and on the grounds outside the Alamo.

I could hear the conversation between Mrs. Locke and the rest of the group over the traffic as I followed the path and rounded the corner. I also heard animals. Wild animals. I was sure I heard an elephant trumpeting, then a lion roaring. My thoughts turned cloudy, like the sky. The last thing I wanted to do was tell Mrs. Locke that I'd heard wild animals.

Once, when Daddy and Mother had gone to see a heart specialist, I awoke in the night, my entire body covered in sweat. I'd dreamt there were so many elephants on the roof of the Scotts' house where I was staying that it was caving in. I hadn't told anyone, but I'd been petrified. Had elephants on the roof been a sign that Daddy was going to die? Did hearing an elephant on the walking path now mean that something would happen to Larry?

"Tyra," George interrupted my spiraling thoughts of doom, "what do you think about the walk and the pond?"

~~~~

EIGHT

Going to the Dining Room

Mrs. Locke was the group escort to the dining room that night. Before going downstairs she took roll, as she had done prior to our walk. Forbes; Skylar, a young, pretty blond who loved to wear white patent leather, knee-high go-go boots; Jonathan, another long-haired kid, wearing a T-shirt with a picture of a surfboard on the back; and I followed Mrs. Locke through the double doors.

"Jonathan, meet Tyra." Mrs. Locke introduced me to the kid with the surfboard on his shirt. "She's joining the group in the dining room for the first time."

"How goes it?" Jonathan replied. The elevator doors closed before I could respond, and we were on our way.

Jonathan and I stepped out of the elevator together. "See you later," he said as he walked toward the dining room. "I eat on my own. Graduated. You know . . . I come and go by myself as long as I check in and out."

I was jealous of his freedom. If I could just eat a meal without throwing up, it would be a major step toward getting well. In the cafeteria, I would have to make choices, select which food to eat. I felt disgusted that such a basic decision caused me so much anxiety.

Large picture windows filled most of the back wall of the dining room, inviting us to dine on the patio outside. *Beautiful*, I thought. On the walls between the windows, modern paintings in bright colors warmed the room. Strong and bold, they were a testament to the inner strength and passion of their creators. I wondered if patients had painted them.

We ate in the same room as our doctors, nurses, and the rest of the hospital staff and guests of the Clinic. Patients sat at some of the tables, staff sat at others, and at a few more tables, patients and staff intermingled. The dining room had a sophisticated air, not so much from the furniture as because of the way people acted. We had earned the privilege to eat there and enjoyed a certain status that came with it. Our behavior was on display. Those who couldn't handle the responsibility ate on their units.

"Since it's the weekend, it's not as crowded. Not as many doctors and staff on duty," George explained, as he motioned for me to follow him.

The serving line reminded me of Furr's Cafeteria in Lubbock. My grandmother Nennie used to come to Lubbock on business once or twice a month. She'd always made it a point to take Larry and me out to lunch. "It's on me,'" she'd smile, aware that we were both going to school and working. "All you can eat."

The servers at Menninger were friendly. Some noticed I was new and went out of their way to explain what the choices were.

"Desserts are great here," George offered with excitement. "Save room."

Right, I thought to myself, trembling. *God, please let me be like everybody else, not loving and hating food at the same time. Help me act like a normal person.* Food called to me, mouthwatering and beautiful, the sustenance of life. But once I swallowed it, it felt rotten in the pit of my stomach until I got rid of it.

The manager of the dining room stood at the beginning of the serving line. He introduced himself to me and exchanged greetings and small talk with the other patients.

"Help yourself. If there's anything you need or want, let us know. Enjoy." He spoke like he was family to both patients and staff.

The atmosphere felt a bit like Nennie's house on a holiday, when food was bountiful and PaPa, my grandfather, began all our meals with a prayer. But those days were gone. PaPa had been killed in a tractor accident eight years earlier.

The choices for dinner were overwhelming. Some of my favorite entrees were on the menu: hamburger steaks, spaghetti with meat sauce, and broiled fish. There were others I didn't recognize. I chose the hamburger steak and moved on to the vegetables. Creamed spinach caught my eye. I added it to my tray. Spinach had been a favorite since I was five. In elementary school, I'd had all the spinach I could eat, since none of the other kids liked it.

As I moved along the line, I could barely focus on the entrees, side dishes, or condiments. The desserts loomed at the end. I grew queasy. When George said he planned to come back for dessert after he finished his entree, I could have hugged him. I hadn't thought of postponing my pie decision. I was safe, for the moment.

We joined the group table. I pulled my chair up next to Skylar's. She struggled to participate in the conversation with the rest of us, a forced smile on her face. Skylar's food went in her mouth, slowly came back out on the end of her tongue and disappeared again. Then she swallowed. As soon as she put more food in her mouth, her tongue came out again, like a clock's cuckoo. I hadn't seen anyone eat like that since Laura first ate baby cereal and strained peaches.

Some patients said Skylar had a tongue thrust because she was scared and insecure. They said it soothed her. We all acted like we didn't notice. We all had our own idiosyncrasies. I wondered if the others diagnosed me when I wasn't around. As far as I knew, no one had discovered that I could gorge a whole pie topped with a can of whipped cream or a pint of ice cream, then vomit.

Mrs. Locke, seated next to George, was working during dinner. She brought up subjects for discussion that were clearly topics of

interest to certain patients. She worked hard to encourage everyone to participate in the conversation. I had little to say, though
I did my best to act confident and comfortable at the table. But I
worried about the decision I still had to make.

While I was on trays, I had been afraid to eat dessert. I thought
if I ate only one piece of pie or cake or one dish of ice cream, I'd
need another. If I couldn't have another, my nose would burn out
of control. I could have asked for more, but then the staff would
know I had eaten more than one and make a note of it in my chart.
Besides, two servings wouldn't have been enough. There was never
enough to stop the need, unless I stuffed myself to the gills then
slept, drugged by food and protected from constant fear. If I suc-
cumbed to one dessert, I would feel crazy. I had no tools—no razor
blades and not enough food in my stomach to purge, nothing to
stop the horrific anxiety.

I consoled myself with the thought that they had all three of my
favorite pies in the dining room: coconut, chocolate, and pumpkin. I promised myself that I would take just one. I selected a piece
of coconut cream. As long as I ate it with the group, I wouldn't
have the nerve to eat another slice. The group would protect me
from myself.

NINE

The Rose Garden

I slept through the first day of morning classes, ate lunch with the group, then went up to my room and lay back down on my bed. Staring at Larry and Laura's photos, I wondered if we'd ever be together again. *Maybe I'll get a letter from Larry this afternoon*, I thought, trying to remember exactly what he and Laura looked like.

A knock on my door woke me around 3:00 that afternoon. Just as I'd thought, it was Dr. Roberts. I was always relieved when he showed up. I trusted him and felt safe when I was with him. We went to the dining room for coffee then headed outdoors for a walk. "I understand you didn't go to classes this morning," Dr. Roberts said.

Defensive and still groggy, I quipped, "Didn't wake up on time."

"Don't you have an alarm clock? I understood you to say you did," he challenged.

"Forgot to set it," I mumbled.

"Do you want one of the aides to remind you?"

"No, I can remember." I didn't hide my irritation.

"Here we are." We entered the rose garden. Dr. Roberts stopped beside two metal chairs. "We're having an Indian summer. It's October, and the roses are still blooming."

A small metal plate labeled with the botanical name of each rose bush was stuck in the dirt at the base of each plant. They reminded me of the temporary nameplates that are used at the cemetery until a permanent stone marker is put in place.

"I don't like roses. I don't want to sit in here," I announced.

Dr. Roberts moved the two metal chairs outside the garden. "What don't you like about the rose garden?"

"I don't want to sit here, either. I want to keep walking," I said. "The rose garden reminds me of Daddy and death." The beauty of the full blooms in reds, bright and soft pinks, yellows, and whites was an affront. To me, roses meant loss. They reminded me of the passing of so many loved ones and of the prospect of the death I dreaded most, the possibility that Larry would die in Vietnam.

"Tell me more," Dr. Roberts encouraged as we walked.

"When I see all these perfect roses I think of death and funerals. I'd never seen so many perfect roses in one place, until my baby cousin drowned when I was six. Then Daddy died, and a year later Pa Decker, his daddy, went, too. Five years later, Daddy's brother, Uncle Frank, died. They all died of heart attacks. PaPa Sexton, Mother's daddy, died in a tractor accident the same year Uncle Frank died. The day Laura was born, my twenty-year-old cousin ran her car into a tree and was killed. Roses make me sick to my stomach."

By the time I finished the litany of all the deaths in my family, we were back at the hospital. Dr. Roberts walked me to my room. "I know you feel sad. You have reason to," he said. "We can talk about this again. Remember, you're strong," he encouraged.

~~~~

When my alarm rang the next morning, I woke to the crazy half-dream state of impending doom that was typical of all my mornings. I rolled over, closed my eyes, and went back to sleep.

Knocking interrupted my escape. I jumped up, unsteady and dazed.

"Mrs. Hull." The knocking grew louder. It was Dr. Roberts again. "Mrs. Hull?"

I was still in my pajamas. I couldn't answer that way. In a sleepy stupor, I stared at the door but didn't budge. Dr. Roberts persisted. "Mrs. Hull." He knocked again and again. "I've come to take you to class."

"I'm coming," I finally called, throwing on a robe before I opened the door.

"Get ready for class." Dr. Roberts didn't react negatively when he saw me in my pajamas. "I'll wait outside and walk you over when you're dressed."

I rummaged through my closet and grabbed a polyester pantsuit. I stared at my face in the utility mirror above the small sink in the bathroom. *No way you have time for eyeliner*, I thought, thrown off guard and nervous about Dr. Roberts waiting outside. I combed my hair and went out the door. "I don't look ready, and I didn't have time for makeup," I apologized.

A smile flickered on the doctor's face. I got the sense that Dr. Roberts and I were allies, but he was not a pushover. "You look fine," he assured me. These classes are important to your treatment. You must go regularly.

"I'll walk you over to sewing and introduce you to the instructor," he said. "Then you'll go to gym. Once a week, you'll have piano lessons with Polly. Save any questions for this afternoon. I'll see you when you get back from gym."

Dr. Roberts really cared. Cutting classes as I had in high school wasn't an option here. I didn't want another day of being escorted to class or attending without makeup. I was determined to do better, no matter how early I had to set my alarm to get up on time.

When we arrived at the sewing room, Dr. Roberts introduced me to the teacher Mona, who was helping a patient hem a garment. She pulled out three or four rolls of fabric and told me to select one for my project. I wasn't crazy about sewing, so I randomly picked a striped pattern. Mother's voice chided in my head:

"It's good for you to do things you don't like to do. Good training for life."

When class ended, Mona escorted me outside, down the well-manicured path to the gymnasium. Patients were playing volleyball as "Joy to the World" by Three Dog Night, one of my favorite bands, blared over the loudspeaker.

The musical notes and a tiny shiver of happiness pulsed down my spine. It was an emotion I hadn't felt in months. One Menninger staffer later told me music was good therapy, except for country music. He said it was too depressing. I believed that, for sure. I'd spent countless hours as a teenager singing into a hairbrush, imitating Patsy Cline singing her hit "Crazy," and look where I'd ended up.

Though I didn't like physical activity, I was pleased to recognize some of the patients, especially George, Deborah, and Lainey, lined up at the volleyball net.

"Over here, Mrs. Hull." A thirtyish African-American man wearing a green Menninger T-shirt and a wide grin pointed to a spot on the court next to the net. "I'm Kyle, your instructor."

Feeling anxious, I joined the group and missed the first volley that came my way.

Although I felt like a klutz, gym turned out to be my favorite class. I loved hearing "Joy to the World" and hummed the tune almost every time I went. I got to know friends on my unit. Forbes was elegant even in his gym clothes. He was a true gentleman and reminded me of Daddy. Forbes took it upon himself to teach me to serve the volleyball.

Soon after that first day of classes, I made it a point to sit in the dining room with Forbes, Lainey, and Deborah. I became close to this group of patients. We had many of the same privileges and were frequently on group together. I ate with them often and joined them on supervised shopping trips to White Lakes Mall.

Mrs. Locke, Forbes, and Lainey would often set up a card table in the hallway for a game of bridge. I was flattered when Forbes and Mrs. Locke offered to teach me to play one day. No one I knew played bridge. The only card games I played were canasta and forty-two. My brother and I had played them with Maw Maw Decker, my daddy's mother, whenever we visited. She also let us drink coffee, even though we were just kids. Maw Maw was a tough card player. She showed us no mercy and almost always won. If Mother could have seen me playing cards at Menninger, she would have said, "I bet you thought you were in high cotton when you were invited to play bridge."

One day while we were playing cards, Forbes announced, "I took time off from my business for one year to come here. When my time is up, I'm going back to work." Forbes was an architect from the West Coast. Before I arrived, I would have thought one year of hospitalization was an extraordinarily long time. But one of the disconcerting discoveries I had made was that one woman had been at Menninger for seven years. It gnawed at me. Larry and I planned to meet in Hawaii for R&R once he received clearance. I had promised to get better and meet him on the beach where the water meets the sand. I'd already told Dr. Roberts I had a date with Larry for R&R. I tried not to dwell on it, but it was frightening to think that I might be at Menninger indefinitely.

I had heard that Dr. Karl Menninger had said that, with treatment, patients could become "weller than well." I understood this to mean some of us would leave healthier than we had ever been. I decided my group of new friends and I were the weller-than-well group. Our illnesses were not as observable as some of the others, like Cassandra, a beautiful young woman who often sat rocking cross-legged on the floor of the patient lounge muttering, "In my mind's eye, in my mind's eye," over and over again.

At Menninger, I observed that human beings develop a pecking order. Ours was based on a privilege hierarchy: Were you well enough to eat on your own, or did you eat with a supervised group, or on the unit on trays? Did you demonstrate grotesque or undesirable behavioral symptoms, or were your symptoms hidden? Could you carry on an intelligent conversation, or did you speak incoherently or in gibberish? Were you neatly dressed, clean, and put together, or did you have body odor, mismatched clothes, and food stains on your clothing?

Mother had been wrong when she'd said the least you can do is look right and act right. Some patients weren't able to look right and act right. That put them at the bottom of the pecking order. Those who could were at the top. Our symptoms were masked by socially acceptable behaviors. I vowed to leave Menninger weller than well. I could hear Larry's voice on one of the cassettes he had sent me: "Do your best and do what the doctors tell you, so you can take care of Laura. I believe in you, and I love you." I would graduate from Menninger, my own peculiar kind of finishing school, with honors. I would leave Menninger weller than well.

Over the next few weeks, I was able to keep my promise to myself to show up for classes and do everything I could to get better, even though it meant I had to set my alarm an extra hour early to have enough time to cajole myself to get out of bed. Dr. Roberts had said attending classes was one of the most important components of my treatment plan. I vowed to be a model patient and do everything he recommended. Meeting Larry in Hawaii was my goal. True to his word, Dr. Roberts added an art class to my daily schedule. Kyle, the volleyball teacher, was also the art instructor.

"So what's your pleasure, clay, painting, jewelry? Or do you have another idea?" he asked. "Feel free to look around at the art displays created by other patients. Here's a great-looking collage one patient made."

"I can't decide between clay or painting. Do you have finger paint?" The last time I had felt like a real artist was in second grade. Over the years, I'd avoided art classes, convinced my efforts were simplistic and no good.

"Yes, ma'am, we have finger paint, but have you worked with clay before?" He pulled a ball of it, twice the size of my fist, out from a cabinet below the wooden work surface. "If you have, you know how easy it is to start over if you change your mind and decide to make something different. Some people don't make anything. They simply like the feel of clay. They work it and mold it during class one day and start over the next. It's up to you. Finger painting's nice but not a great choice if you want to work on a project over a period of days or weeks," he explained.

I chose clay and spent several classes slamming it on the table, stretching it, smashing it flat, balling it up, and rolling the lopsided oval across the square worktable. I would catch it just before it fell to its death. As I worked the clay in my hands, I thought back to second grade, the year I'd overheard my aunts and uncles talking about how Daddy's doctors believed he was going to die if they didn't find a cure.

~~~

Miss Talbert, my second grade teacher, had found me crying on the playground one day after school and invited me to finger paint in her classroom while I waited for the bus. I was staying at the Scotts' while my parents were in Galveston seeing another doctor. Miss Talbert encouraged me to choose from all the colors, though she often used black when she showed us how to use our fingers and forearms to create paintings.

She poured two large capfuls of buttermilk onto the paper.

"Buttermilk causes the paint to spread smoothly on the page

and keeps it from cracking so much as it dries," she explained, as I smeared the liquid with my forearm from the wrist all the way up to my elbow. It felt better than making mud pies.

I painted endless pictures of irises, all of them black. My grandmother Nennie, a self-taught interior decorator, was always appreciative of anything I made with my own hands. One of the irises I painted stood out among the rest, so I decided to give it to her for Mother's Day. Miss Talbert suggested I make a construction paper mat for it. I chose lime green. After wrapping Nennie's surprise in special paper purchased from the Ben Franklin, I counted the days until I could give it to her.

On Mother's Day morning, Daddy, Mother, Rodney, and I drove to Nennie and PaPa's farm. Nennie loved it when we all gathered at their house. Including all the aunts, uncles, and cousins, there were at least fifteen of us. After dinner, while Nennie was opening gifts, I squeezed in between her and the sofa arm, snuggling close. As she bent down to hug me, I whispered, "I have my own gift for you. It's a secret."

Nennie finished unwrapping her gifts, then she announced that she and I had some private business. I retrieved my surprise from the car, and we went into her bedroom. Nennie scooted down to one end of the bed and patted the space beside her. I handed her the wrapped painting as she helped me onto the four-poster bed. I thought I would lose my mind with anticipation. I was elated with my iris and knew Nennie would be, too. I scooted closer to her as she painstakingly removed the wrapping.

"Oh my!" Nennie looked down at my gift. A broad-leafed, tall-stemmed iris completely covered the page. Nennie carefully leaned it against the headboard then pulled me onto her lap. "Tyra, what a wonderful flower! So tall and straight."

"Nennie, it's an iris. Can you see the tiny lines in the leaves? I made them by putting my whole arm in the paint!" I rushed on, eager to tell her about it. "The little hairs on my arms made the tiny lines, like veins in the leaves."

"I do see them, of course. I love it, and I love you." Nennie beamed. "Thank you for making me a gift with your own two hands. This painting is beautiful and will hang in the hallway for everyone to see. When the irises aren't in bloom, I'll have yours to enjoy and think of all the colors it could be."

Nennie paused, and then said, "Tyra, my prayer for you is that someday you will see irises in all the colors of the rainbow. Someday you'll paint irises in greens, purples, reds, and yellows. I love this iris you made for me with black strong leaves and tiny lines etched by the hairs in your arms with a light-gray background. One day, this tiny red flower in the center will grow larger than this whole painting. Until then, this is the best iris I have ever gotten."

As I pounded, stretched, and beat the clay in art class at Menninger, I remembered how Nennie had always been there for me. She had a way of making me feel as if I were just right and not a problem. I'd stayed with her and PaPa during the summers when

Mother and Daddy left home, looking for a cure. She was the first one in my family to embrace Larry and our plans to marry. She told me stories about growing up as a little girl on the prairie when times were hard, and she took me shopping at elegant stores for new clothes. Nennie couldn't make up for the homesickness I felt when Mother and Daddy were gone, or my grief when Daddy died, but she helped me believe we would be all right. As I grew older, I lost the ability to believe her, though I still loved the fact that she tried to make me hopeful.

I could have chosen finger paint, I reminded myself as I struggled during several classes to work the clay into a copy of my own clenched fist, a symbol of my determination. In the end, I was glad I had chosen clay. When it was finished, I put the fist on my small table next to the photos of Larry and Laura. It reminded me to believe in myself—to believe I had what it took to get well.

TEN

Lions and Tigers

Sometimes, time flew by, and sometimes, it dragged on, alternately and mysteriously during the first five weeks I lived at the Clinic. I stayed busy attending classes, having sessions with Dr. Roberts at 3:00, taking walks on the grounds with the group, and making visits to the canteen. A standing chess match with The Minister before dinner around 4:30 was typical, unless I was having an unusually difficult day. I watched the clock during afternoon gym and weekly piano classes, hoping there would be a letter from Larry waiting for me when I returned to the floor. I prayed fiercely, making more promises than even God could have remembered in exchange for Him sending Larry home safely.

I also hoped for letters from Laura's sitter, Marjorie. I loved to hear about the words my daughter had learned and the games she liked to play. At the same time, those letters filled me with sadness. Larry and I were missing so many new firsts in Laura's life. What did she think about our absence? Did she know we missed her, loved her, and longed to be with her? Did she know we both had to be away, that we had no choice? I feared she would never forgive us.

Even though my evenings were full if I took advantage of the opportunities to be with other people, dinner was still a challenge. Confronting the scrumptious desserts prepared by the cafeteria staff continued to be traumatic. After dinner, I filled time attempting to learn bridge, holding chat sessions with Mrs. Locke or one of the other aides on duty, and gossiping with members of the weller-than-well group. Some nights, I accompanied George on the piano while he sang "The Old Lamplighter" repeatedly, until rebellion broke out among the other patients.

One night, shortly after a new patient named Trudi arrived on the floor, she emerged from her room for the 8:00 evening snack cart from the cafeteria. The cart was piled with oranges, pickles, cold cuts, and bread, but there were no serving utensils. Styrofoam cups contained condiments, and tongue depressors replaced silverware. No sharp utensils or glass containers were allowed on the floor among patients. The potential for hurting one's self was too risky.

"Egg salad. Where's the egg salad?" Trudi ordered, rummaging through the items on the cart.

Something about Trudi called to my better self. Her body was short and stocky, and she was unsteady on her feet, as if she could fall over at any moment. She seemed lonely and disoriented in her new surroundings. I took a Styrofoam cup, dropped in a boiled egg, and added globs of mayonnaise and mustard. I mashed the concoction into a lumpy mixture with a tongue depressor, spread it onto a piece of bread, and served it to Trudi on a paper plate. Appreciation sparkled in her eyes as she bit into her treasured favorite. From then on, every night when the snack cart was wheeled out, Trudi shuffled over to me. No matter what I was doing, she'd announce that it was time for an egg salad sandwich.

Despite my kindness toward Trudi, I didn't always feel as if my efforts to participate at Menninger benefited anyone, including myself. My progress was sporadic, evidenced by a difficult conversation with Dr. Roberts during one of our afternoon sessions.

"Mrs. Hull," he began, "one of the servers in the cafeteria

reported observing you taking a slice of pie, hiding it under your jacket, and walking out of the cafeteria. Is that accurate?"

Humiliated, I nodded. *I can't believe even the cafeteria workers report you*, I thought. *Nothing is private here.*

"You don't have to hide food. You're welcome to take as much as you want. Also, the maids who clean your room have reported that your bathroom is splattered with vomit, including the commode, floor, and walls. They have requested that we put a toilet bowl brush and cleaning supplies in your bathroom so you can clean it yourself. They'll be happy to clean your toilet area when you stop vomiting."

I thought I would die from embarrassment as I muttered a soft, "I'm sorry."

"You're not in trouble," he assured me. "Do you want to talk about it?"

"No." I shook my head.

"Another time, then," Dr. Roberts said. "They'll leave the toilet brush and cleaning materials tomorrow, and you'll clean your own toilet."

So much for privacy here, I thought. I was angrier with myself than with the servers and the maids.

"Dr. Roberts, I don't want to talk anymore today," I muttered.

After he left, I stayed in my room feeling like a failure and a piece of shit. Not long after, Mrs. Locke stopped by.

"May I come in?" she asked as she knocked and entered my room. "Hard day, I understand. How about a walk, just you and me?

"That sounds good," I answered. "It has been a tough day."

"It's not unusual to have a setback," she assured. "Does a walk down to the pond sound good? You'll need a coat."

Once we were on the path toward the pond, she asked, "Want to talk about it?"

I shook my head.

"Okay then, let's enjoy our walk."

When we got to the pond, Mrs. Locke sat down in a metal chair and patted the one beside her. "Sit. Let's listen to the quiet."

We sat awhile, then I heard a loud roar, but I said nothing.

"Did you hear that?" Mrs. Locke asked. "When the traffic's not loud, you can hear the animals across the street. Especially when it's close to feeding time."

"Are you kidding me?" I jumped up, excited. "Where are they? On my first group walk, I thought I heard big cats and even an elephant. I thought I was losing it, so I didn't tell anyone."

Mrs. Locke's eyes twinkled. Stifling a chuckle, she said, "Mrs. Hull, there's a zoo across the street from the pond. You didn't know that?"

"No. Thank God!" I giggled. "I thought I was getting sicker after I arrived here."

"You're doing fine. You promised to tell me all about Larry," she said. "This seems like a good time."

I sat down again. "With Thanksgiving around the corner, I've been thinking a lot about Larry and our first Thanksgiving together. After our first date, Larry and I were inseparable. We went to a few Sigma Chi parties but preferred to spend most of our time alone, just the two of us."

Mrs. Locke nodded.

"We found most of our peers kind of immature, although I was only a college freshman and Larry a sophomore," I explained. "Most kids our age seemed out of touch with the things that mattered most to us, like planning our future and realizing our dreams. It was as if each of us had found a missing part of ourselves in the other."

"Go on," Mrs. Locke encouraged.

"I grew up fast after losing Daddy. My baby sister was born

three months later, and my brother and I took care of her while Mother went back to college. I did most of the babysitting, the diaper changing, and the feedings. From then on, my relationship with Mother was skewed. I was more like her partner than her daughter."

Mrs. Locke listened as I recalled how scared I'd been back then. Mother was going to school to be a teacher and make money to take care of us. I wanted to help her make everything better.

"She struggled to raise the three of us kids, build the house she and Daddy had planned to build, and start her new teaching job. I missed Daddy. I was so angry about losing him. I think that's why I was so rebellious as a teenager.

"The year we started dating, Larry invited me to spend Thanksgiving with his family on the air force base in Roswell, New Mexico. His dad was stationed in Thailand. My father had been in the Army Air Corps in WWII, and my favorite photograph of him showed him in his military uniform. I thought Mother would be pleased that I was dating someone who wanted to serve in the armed forces like Daddy. But she wasn't happy when Larry and I started dating."

I tried hard to keep the disappointment out of my voice, but it must have come through, because Mrs. Locke patted my arm.

"When I drove up to the gate at the base on Thanksgiving, I saw Larry's '57 Chevy waiting on the other side. As the guard motioned me forward past the barrier, a huge knot in my throat warned me something big was happening. I could hardly breathe. The flags and the MPs filled me with awe and anticipation, but there was also this fear. When the guard waved me through the gate, it was as if the road to my life opened ahead of me. We were on that road, Larry, the United States Air Force, and me."

Tears welled in my eyes.

"When we pulled up in front of the house," I continued, "Larry's mother was standing on the front porch waiting for us. Larry jumped out of his car, opened my door, and led me to the porch.

"'Here she is,' he grinned.

"Mrs. Hull put her arms around me in a warm, tight hug. She said that Larry had told her all about me and what I liked to eat. She had made some of my favorites for dinner."

"Oh, my," Mrs. Locke clapped her hands together. "I can see why he's 'Your Larry,' as you refer to him. And his mother, cooking all your favorite foods, and him remembering them all and telling her! That is some special young man. No wonder you miss him, and his mother, too!"

"I was touched that Larry had kept track of what I liked to eat. Mrs. Hull had prepared celery stuffed with cream cheese and chives, pumpkin pie with whipped cream, and hot, strong coffee. After we ate, Larry and his mom washed dishes while I sat at the kitchen table, listening to them tell stories about living on the base in Japan and about Mrs. Hull's relatives in Alabama. She told me that when I met her relatives, it would be like they had always known me, because I was with Larry and they all just loved him. *Who didn't love Larry*, I wondered to myself."

Mrs. Locke smiled.

"I admired the relationship between Larry and his mother," I went on. "There was a sweetness and respect between the two of them, a kind of harmony that made being around them comfortable and easy. It was very different from my family. After a holiday meal, the men in my family left the table to play dominoes, tell stories, or have a smoke while the women cleaned up. I couldn't remember feeling so much at home in a long time. I'd been falling in love with Larry over the past couple of months. That visit to his family's left me utterly smitten."

"I can see why. Who wouldn't be?" Mrs. Locke agreed.

"Christmas was coming up. I hadn't liked the holidays since Daddy died. But now, there was something to look forward to again."

"It's clear this husband of yours is one special young man. You have every right to be proud of him," she said.

Mrs. Locke stood up. "Mrs. Hull, this has been a full day. You must be tired," she comforted. "Let's get back and join the group for dinner."

We walked around the pond and headed for the hospital. The day had been difficult, but I couldn't help grinning from ear to ear.

"What's that smile all about?" Mrs. Locke asked.

"I'm not hearing things," I said. "There's a zoo across the street."

ELEVEN

Keep Dealin'

Mother and her closest friend, Lynette, made the twelve-hour drive to visit me the Friday after Thanksgiving. I had mixed feelings about them coming, even though I told Dr. Roberts I wanted them to come when he asked how I felt about it. I feared that seeing Mother might pull me back into the awful depression and anxiety I'd felt when I lived with her. The thought of her visiting made me miss Larry and Laura even more. *Too bad I couldn't choose them to come instead of her.* The thought made me feel guilty.

Dr. Roberts had written an order for Mother to pick me up for dinner Saturday evening. I met her and Lynette in the circle drive, and we went to a steakhouse at White Lakes Mall. I felt nervous and unsure of myself. I worried about how Mother thought I was doing. Mrs. Locke had told me that some patients found the first family visit after hospitalization uncomfortable. My world at the Clinic was small, predictable, and safe. Leaving the hospital grounds didn't fulfill my fantasies of being free to come and go on my own. It felt threatening more than liberating.

Mother filled me in on Laura's visits to Seminole. I was pleased that she and my younger sister took Laura home with them for holidays and on some weekends, yet, to my dismay, a jolt of jealousy flashed through me. I would have given anything to see my baby girl.

During dinner we discussed our letters from Larry and compared notes on Marjorie's reports of Laura's progress, such as my baby's new favorite foods and books, and new words she had learned. Mother wanted to know about the classes I was taking and the friends I had made. I had the feeling she'd been given a list of topics she could talk about and others to avoid. I didn't know what to say to her. The description of my activities felt tedious and forced, and her enthusiastic responses inappropriate, given how little I was doing compared to my earlier studies at Texas Tech. But I supposed that for Mom, hearing that I was getting up and out of bed and following the prescribed routine was a big deal. I wanted to go back to the ward. I had more in common with the other patients than with my own family. An unspoken acceptance among those of us on the ward made me feel safe. It didn't require attendance at a certain church or believing in a certain way. You weren't out just because you didn't fit in. Though we all had a diagnosis that demonstrated we belonged at the Clinic, hope was in the air.

I followed the clock on the wall above the salad bar, watching the minutes of my three-hour leave tick by. They seemed to go so slowly.

"Dinner has passed so fast. We barely have an hour before I need to have you back at the Clinic." Mother sounded sad.

"It's the same rules for everybody," I explained. "It's the first time I've left the campus without a hospital escort." *You'll be sorry you eyed the clock all night*, I told myself. *Tomorrow morning, you'll wake up and she'll be gone. You'll worry she'll have an accident, and that you didn't make the most of your time with her. Don't you know better by now?*

~~~

The weller-than-well group was into a game of bridge at a card table in the hallway across from the nurses' station when I arrived back on the unit.

"Come over here and take my hand," Mrs. Locke waved her

cards. "I'll coach you," she offered, pulling an extra chair up next to her. "Sit here. Lainey and I are partners. You'll be Forbes's partner."

Deborah sat at the table, observing. As I scooted my chair next to her, she leaned over and whispered, "Difficult night for Skylar. She's been screaming a lot. Two or three aides are in there with her. She's in wet sheets. Must be cooled down by now, I haven't heard her for a while."

"Too bad about Skylar," I muttered to Deborah. Skylar's very bad days sometimes included being wrapped in wet sheets. She must have felt she was in bondage. Once she got free, she would run toward the far end of the hall, where the "angel of heaven," a nurse dressed in all white, would rescue her from the "terrible evil men" who had held her down. If she could just get to the angel, she'd be saved.

I'd been saved right after Daddy died, so someday I could be with him in heaven. But I hadn't felt the way the preacher said you were supposed to feel, so I kept going down to the pulpit every time the invitation to rededicate your life was given. Mother finally suggested I quit going.

"All right now," Mrs. Locke interrupted. "Let's go over what you learned last time. As we got into the swing of the game, I wondered whether Mother had detected my discomfort at dinner and my desire to get back to the unit. I hoped not.

"Tyra, it's your deal." Mrs. Locke nudged me. Just then, Skylar's door flung open. She ran stark naked past our table and the nurses' station, screaming as she rounded the corner and headed toward her "angel" at the other end of the hall. Two aides followed at full speed.

Trudi, who was standing by the snack cart with a half-chewed carrot hanging out of her mouth, announced, "It's a hell of a hospital, a hell of a country club, a hell of a hospital, right?"

Forbes didn't miss a beat. "Keep dealin', Tyra. Just keep dealin'."

TWELVE

Silent Night

The Clinic staff went out of their way to make Christmastime special. But it was a mental hospital, and protocol still had to be enforced. I opened presents in my room Christmas morning supervised by an aide. She handed me a pair of scissors to cut through the cardboard packages. I suspected she also made mental notes, then returned to the nurses' station to record what I received, my comments, and state of mind after opening my gifts. It was not unusual for letters or contact from family members to evoke distress, homesickness, and a multitude of other complex feelings in patients. This special day, Christmas, I resented the supervision. It was one of the few times I felt like an inmate, and the reality of living in a locked-down institution bothered me.

I received two pantsuits, one from my mother and one from the Lamberts. I missed Laura desperately. She wasn't even two years old, and she was celebrating the holidays without Larry or me. The photographs Mom and Marjorie sent depicted a somber little girl, not the animated laughing child I remembered. Fear that I might not get well and that Larry might not make it back from Vietnam swelled in me. Dr. Roberts always said, "We have only today." I reminded myself that I had no control over whether Larry lived through the war, just like I couldn't keep Daddy from dying. I recalled my vow to work hard at treatment. I would get better.

After the aide left my room, I tried on my new pantsuits. Both were polyester, one burgundy, the other royal blue. They looked handmade. I grimaced at the thought of wearing one of them to the dining room for Christmas dinner. At the same time, I felt compelled to choose something new for such a special occasion, since I was sure the other patients would dress up. A wave of shame at my lack of appreciation swept over me, and I was overcome by homesickness.

Like a nostalgic movie, memories of my father's last Christmas played in my head. Our tradition included driving forty miles to my maternal grandparents' farm on Christmas Eve after Daddy got off work. Each year, immediately after lunch, my brother and I began pestering our mother. We grew frenzied with anticipation. "Everyone is probably already there. We're going to miss the fireworks!" After fireworks, Santa Claus arrived at Nennie and PaPa's. He personally handed out beautifully wrapped gifts, each inscribed with our names. As a small girl, I'd felt bad for PaPa. Just before Santa arrived, he had to go to the barn to milk and feed the cows. By age six, I was wise to Santa's true identity.

When Daddy finally arrived home that last year we were all together, Rodney and I helped Mother pack the car while Daddy took off his coat and tie. The drive to the farm seemed to take forever. Burl Ives and Gene Autry sang carols like "Holly Jolly Christmas" and "Rudolph the Red Nosed Reindeer" on the radio. Bing Crosby's "White Christmas" was my favorite. I had never seen a white Christmas and fantasized that snow turned the world into a true winter wonderland.

Just as Daddy turned the car off the highway onto the four-mile, red dirt road to Nennie and PaPa's house, he said to Mother in a deliberately loud voice that he was almost positive he could see a streak of light just to the right of the moon. It was undoubtedly Santa's sleigh, led by Rudolph.

My thirteen-year-old brother responded with typical teenage cynicism, while I craned my neck and peered out the back window. The banter continued as I snuggled deeper into my blanket in the corner of the back seat. We were a real family, together on Christmas Eve. Stars sparkled across the night sky. The huge silvery moon evoked a sense of peace. I knew there was no Santa or reindeer up there, but maybe God was. Maybe God would make Daddy well for Christmas. That was all I wanted. But the Christmas of 1955 turned out to be my father's last.

God hadn't taken care of Daddy. Why should I think He would take care of Larry?

I had to leave my room and go be with people before I got too caught up in Christmases past. I dressed in my royal blue pantsuit and put on some makeup, then walked down to the patient lounge.

The patients gathered in the lounge just as my family had gathered in Nennie's living room before Christmas dinner. I sat down on the sofa next to the minister's wife, who was no relation to The Minister on the unit. We exchanged pleasantries while Cassandra, dressed beautifully in angelic white, perched cross-legged on the other side of me, chattering about how God was indeed real, especially on Christmas.

As I had imagined, everyone had dressed for the occasion. Forbes, Lainey, Deborah, Skylar, George, Trudi, and Mrs. Locke all eventually appeared. I was disappointed but not surprised to see that The Minister had stayed in his room. I seldom saw him, except for our regularly scheduled chess match before dinner most days.

I could not recall ever seeing so many patients in the lounge. Even Mrs. Rupert was there. She would go with us to the dining room just for this special occasion. On bad days, Mrs. Rupert applied a week's worth of rouge to her cheeks, so having her in the group was like having our own personal clown for dinner. Despair betrayed her painted rosy cheeks and lipstick smile as it poured from her tormented eyes.

Jonathan, our own California surfer boy who had introduced me to the Rolling Stones, usually stayed in his room listening to his newest album on his personal hi-fi, but today he came to the lounge, too.

Becky didn't join us for Christmas dinner. In the eight months I spent at Menninger, I never saw her come out of her room next to the nurses' station. She frequently stood in the shadows behind her partially opened door. Once, she stepped into the light of the doorway and stared down at my feet as I walked by. Her hair was uncombed, and her clothes hung baggy and limp from her shoulders. Crouched by her door, Becky reminded me of a small, frightened animal. I always spoke to her but never got a reply. She never looked at me. I thought she had to be the loneliest, saddest person at Menninger.

The excitement level gained momentum as we were organized into groups to be supervised by nurses' aides. Patients negotiated seat assignments for their group of choice. Groans of disappointment from those unable to sit with their friends reminded me of the teenagers in my family when they were informed there was no room for them at the grown-ups' table. Chatter about the anticipated Christmas menu added to the commotion. Finally, it was time to take the elevator downstairs.

The dining room was magnificent; the meal, a feast fit for the holiday. Round tables were decorated with festive sparkling decorations. Christmas was in the air. Even those patients whose faces were typically draped in sadness or showed no signs of emotion seemed more animated.

I missed Larry, Laura, Mother, and Nennie, as well as the troop of relatives we always saw over the holidays. Conversation focused on the food, the family traditions of those at the table, and stories of their best Christmases ever. One of the diners was Jewish. It was the first time I heard why Hanukkah was celebrated.

By the time dessert was served, I was feeling right at home. The cherries jubilee, a scrumptious dish I had never heard of, much less tasted, was something I could get used to. I determined to have it again after I was released.

Dinner was lovely, even with tongue thrusters and those who stirred the food on their plates into unappetizing gobs. It didn't matter; most everyone who could come to the dining room was there. These patients were my family for now, and I belonged.

Laura was with Mother, so she'd have presents to open and mashed potatoes, dressing, and gravy to eat. I wondered what Larry was having for Christmas dinner. I hoped he would have a nice meal at the officer's club in Da Nang, like the Kobe beef he'd written me about eating when he'd gone to Japan for a short R&R.

~~~

When Larry drove into the yard in front of Nennie's house the Christmas Eve just after we'd started dating, I was thrilled to see him and also petrified that one of my relatives might not be on their best behavior. Luckily, my uncles offered him the West Texas handshake and treated him like a man, not like a twenty-year-old college student. It was a wonderful day. Larry joined my huge extended family at the dinner table, acknowledging my uncles' teasing with just the right amount of deference for a young suitor. Mother wasn't particularly friendly since she thought I was too young to have a serious boyfriend, but she was respectful. That was good enough for me.

Larry beamed as he looked around and took in my grandparents' farm. He was thrilled to be there. I took him on a tour, although there wasn't much to see besides the crops in the field across the road from the house, the old windmill, and tractors and farm equipment parked a ways down behind the house. It was no longer like it had been when I was young, and Nennie and PaPa raised pigs, cows, and a few chickens. Still, life on a farm wearing cowboy boots, riding horses, and shooting West Texas game with relatives was attractive to a young man without roots or a home-town to call his own.

~~~

After dinner, I walked Larry out to his car. I could feel Daddy's presence, and I knew he was proud. Larry had been a hit with most of my family, and it was evident he'd had a good time. As we hugged good-bye, we both recognized that we offered each other the possibility of a new family, a new beginning.

My heart ached for my husband and my daughter as I recalled that first Christmas with Larry. I made a fervent wish that this would be the only year we'd spend the holidays apart. As I rode the elevator back to the unit, I started to cry. "Get a hold of yourself; you can do this," Larry's voice whispered. "Remember, this is just for a while. The three of us will be together again."

I wandered into the tiny patient library feeling lonely and lost on my favorite holiday. As I scanned the shelves, I found a book on how my favorite Christmas carol, "Silent Night," had been written. The organ in St. Nicholas Church in Oberndorf, a small village in the Austrian Alps, had broken down just before Christmas Eve. Franz Gruber and Joseph Mohr set the lyrics for the carol to guitar, providing music for the Christmas service. Finding the story about "Silent Night" felt like a small miracle. It was a nugget of hope when I most needed one, God's gift to me that Christmas.

~~~~~~~~

THIRTEEN

Cutting

After Christmas, I was able to get back into my regular schedule, which helped me feel less homesick for Larry and Laura. I looked forward to my next 3:00 meeting with Dr. Roberts. I had missed him over the long weekend.

"Tell me about the holidays," he said, as we headed to the dining room for our coffee. "Did you enjoy yourself?"

"The food was really good," I replied. "I'd never had cherries jubilee before. It was pretty special."

Dr. Roberts poured two cups of coffee. I suggested we stay inside and sat down at a table next to the windows overlooking the patio.

"Good idea," he agreed. "It's cold today. Tell me more about your Christmas."

"Christmas has always been my favorite holiday, but I hated this one." I started to cry. "Dr. Roberts, what if Larry's plane gets shot down? What if he doesn't come home? I have nightmares about something happening to him. When I was little, I had nightmares about losing Daddy, and then he died. What if the same thing happens to Larry?"

"Mrs. Hull, I can understand your concern for your husband, given his circumstances and the loss of your father at an early age. But your husband is not your father. And you're not a child, as you were then," Dr. Roberts reminded me, his eyes full of compassion.

"Each day the sun comes up, and we do our best. You'll be strong for Laura and for yourself, whatever the future holds.

"Tell me about your fear of losing your father when you were a child," he said.

"When I was seven, I overheard my Aunt Lucille and Uncle Leland say that Daddy was going to die. Daddy had hardening of the arteries. The doctors said he needed to quit smoking and take time off from work, so my parents would go on relaxation trips to Yellowstone or Santa Fe for two or three weeks at a time. Sometimes, they'd just get home from one of those trips and a doctor would call offering Daddy an appointment to try and help him. One time, they regrouped after being home for just two days and drove to Galveston to see the new doctor. I was devastated. I'd marked off the days until my parents would be home on the calendar, but then they were gone again, just like that.

"Sometimes my brother and I stayed with our aunt and uncle when my parents traveled. Other times, when we stayed with friends, we had to be separated. I hated those times the most. I worried constantly about Daddy dying. I knew it was a matter of time." I stopped to take a breath. "Dr. Roberts, the feeling that something awful was going to happen has moved from Daddy to Larry."

"I hear that," he said.

"By the end of third grade," I went on, "I dreaded going home after school. I always looked at the back screen door first. Had Mother pinned a note there? Was today the day, again? The notes she left on the door usually meant another heart emergency. They were directions for my brother and me to go inside and wait until someone came for us. We weren't to go out, in case Mother called. Rodney sometimes had after-school sports. I'd wait for instructions alone, sitting on the living room sofa. I would try to decipher the seriousness of the episode by how messy Mother's handwriting was on the note. I'd walk through the house, looking for clues. If

Mother had time to tidy up, that meant Daddy was not too bad off. If dishes were left in the sink or freshly laundered clothes were still piled unfolded on my parents' bed, I feared the worst. I tried to figure out what was happening from the clues. It made me feel better."

"Why do you think it helped?" Dr. Roberts asked.

"If I could figure out what was happening, I didn't have to worry so much, because I went through what I would do in my head and how I would handle it. Over time, I just imagined the worst. When it didn't happen, I was relieved."

"Some people do that," Dr. Roberts acknowledged. "They hope for the best and plan for the worst. I hear you planning for the worst, but not much hoping for the best. We'll work on that."

"I worried about who would take care of us if Daddy died. My mother was pregnant with my sister. How could we have a new baby if Mother had to go to work?" I threw my hands up, and Dr. Roberts stifled a smile at my exasperation.

"One afternoon, I came home to a note on the door, then the phone rang. It was Mother. She asked me to go get our next-door neighbor. After she got off the phone, Ida Mae said, 'Your daddy has to stay in the hospital for a night or two. He's going to be all right. P. D. and I will take you and Rodney to see him at the hospital after supper.'

"Dr. Roberts, I acted brave, but I was scared. Scared about what was happening. Every day, I was so scared it was the day Daddy would die."

"You were brave and responsible. Your mother trusted you. Not every nine-year-old could be counted on to follow directions," Dr. Roberts encouraged. I hung my head like a child and mumbled, "Thank you." Telling Dr. Roberts all this made me feel sad and lonely all over again.

Returning to my story, I said, "I went to my room and sat down on the floor inside the closet. 'Thank you, God, for not letting

Daddy die,' I prayed. Then I stepped back out and got my crayons and favorite coloring book. I almost never went to the hospital to see Daddy without taking him a gift.

"After Ida Mae served tuna casserole for dinner, she and Paul Darling took us to the hospital. The white linoleum hallway reeked with that awful antiseptic smell. Mrs. Thompson, Daddy's favorite nurse, knew us pretty well by then. She gave me a hug and squeezed my brother's shoulder. 'Your daddy's going to be fine,' she reassured us. 'He's sitting up in bed waiting for you.'

"When we walked in, Daddy was hooked up to all these machines," I recalled. "Mother was standing next to his bed. Daddy smiled and reached out to me. 'Hi, Baby,' he said to me. He asked the nurse if I could sit next to him." I giggled. "He called her 'General Thompson.'

"Nurse Thompson lifted me onto the bed. My brother moved next to Mother. We were always in pairs like that: me and Daddy, Rodney and Mother," I explained. "I handed Daddy the page I had colored and moved closer to him. Nurse Thompson warned me to be careful around the equipment. Rodney glared at me.

"Daddy was okay that time," I sighed. "But what about next time? We pretended it was all good, but we knew one day it would be bad. One day, Daddy would go to the hospital and not come home."

"When a small child's parent is seriously ill and frequently absent, it's normal for the child to be fearful and focused on their parent's health and absence," Dr. Roberts consoled. "In your case, you were sometimes even separated from your whole family, when you and your brother stayed with different people. It was no one's fault. I'm sure those were the most reasonable and supportive arrangements your family had available.

"That doesn't mean it wasn't difficult for you," he acknowledged. "You did your best. You can be proud of that, and also that you had a very special relationship with your father. We'll talk about this again, but you've earned a break for now. This is work, you know. Important work."

~~~~

I saw Dr. Roberts every day that week, as usual. We continued our conversation about loss. For the first time, I had the opportunity to talk to someone about how I'd lost my childhood once I learned my father was dying. Our sessions unearthed the pent-up grief and distress I had buried for over sixteen years. Dr. Roberts had become a father figure, and I trusted him enough to tell him secrets I'd never told anyone.

When Saturday came, he didn't show up for his typical morning check-in. I watched the door to the patient lounge, where I was polishing my shoes. He usually stopped by around 9:00. By 9:30, my nose had started tingling as my anxiety grew stronger. I gathered up the polish and shoes and went to my room, contemplating our last session. I had told him that my greatest fear was that Larry's plane would be shot down and that he would be killed.

I was so agitated I barely got through the day. I slept most of Sunday. By Sunday evening, I couldn't handle the fear of being left alone again. It was too much like feeling abandoned when I was little. Unrelenting thoughts of Larry's plane crashing and burning surged through my brain like electrical currents. My nose burned as if it would explode. Fearful of falling into the darkness, I had to do something.

I moved with purpose into the patient lounge and over to the kitchenette, where the empty soda bottles were stored in wooden crates. I made sure none of the patients or staff were watching as I picked up an empty Tab bottle and hid it under my T-shirt.

I walked back to my room and closed the door. I turned on the radio, so the music would muffle any noise. Kneeling next to the toilet, I cracked the bottle on the tile floor. A large jagged piece of glass broke off. Methodically, I picked it up, turned my left wrist over, and cut three times.

The first cut was ineffective, because I was timid. I grew braver. The third cut was deep. Blood gushed from my wrist. I held my arm over the toilet and watched as the blood ran into the bowl, dissolving from bright red to pink like cherry Kool-Aid in a pitcher of cold water. I stared down into the toilet, hypnotized by the swirling pink clouds, then rested my head on the toilet seat, no longer feeling alone, panicked, or crazy. A languid tranquility lingered. I felt at peace, just like "the peace that passeth all understanding" from the scripture the preacher read when I was a child.

Until reality asserted itself again.

Blood was dripping fast.

I had to tell someone.

I put on a long-sleeve shirt, held my arm close to my side, and walked down to the nurses' station looking for Jamie, the nurse I trusted most on the evening shift. I asked her to come to my room, where I showed her my arm. There was no chastising, just quick, sure action as she wrapped a towel around my wrist, stepped out into the hall, and called for an aide to apply pressure to the wound while she went to call Dr. Roberts.

Jamie returned to walk me over to the medical clinic. Even though it was Sunday evening, Dr. Tyne was already there when we arrived. He was his usual kind, compassionate self. He didn't ask too many questions as he stitched my wrist back together and wrapped my arm up to the elbow. He left that aspect of my treatment to Dr. Roberts.

Walking back to the ward, I noticed the twinkle of the stars in the sky. I remembered Larry telling me that whenever I missed him, I should look up and know that on the other side of the world he would be seeing the same moon and stars and thinking about me. I felt a huge sense of remorse for what I had just done to myself.

Dr. Roberts was waiting in my room. He looked painfully tired, his face drawn, as I sat down on the bed. "What happened?" he asked. "What's going on?"

I sobbed and blubbered about my fear of losing Larry, my homesickness, and my longing for Laura. I hadn't seen her for four months. I felt so guilty. Her father was in Vietnam, and her mother was in a mental hospital. Dr. Roberts assured me I was where I belonged and that Laura's life would be better because I would be able to care for her. As far as we knew, Larry was fine. That was all we had today.

When patients hurt themselves, they were placed on "watch." That meant moving all the small pieces of furniture out of their room and locking the dresser drawers and the closet. I would have to ask a staff person to unlock my drawers in the morning so I could get to my clothes and makeup. The bed would be moved out. I would sleep on the mattress on the floor.

"Please, please, don't treat me crazy," I begged through my tears. "If you do, I'll get crazy. I know what I did looks crazy, but it only looks that way. I wasn't trying to kill myself; I just had to stop the pain. That's all! I had to stop the terrible desperate feelings of being alone in the dark with no one to comfort me.

"Dr. Roberts, if you do this, I'll get sicker," I pleaded. "I won't have anything to get better for. I'll see myself as sick. All the other patients will treat me sick. I'll lose all my privileges."

I tried to stay calm, hoping to convince Dr. Roberts that I was okay, but inside me the frenzy was building again. "If you do this, I'm afraid I'll fall apart again. Right now, I'm just barely holding on."

After what seemed like forever, Dr. Roberts finally said he would see if an exception could be made, since this setback wasn't typical of my recent progress. He understood that I had a behavioral compulsion. He also believed that I had been doing better lately. If he kept me off watch, I had to promise that I would tell a staff member if I felt like hurting myself again. If the staff were all busy, I was to sit on my hands on a chair outside the nurses' station until someone could talk with me. I promised, and then I promised some more.

Just before he left he said, "Mrs. Hull, I believe in you."

I started to sob all over again. I cried until I couldn't cry anymore. I laid down and fell asleep. Maybe I could get well if Dr. Roberts believed that I could.

The next morning, when I went down to the patient lounge for coffee, I was horrified to see that all the soda bottles had been removed. A sign had been posted: "Patients, when you want a soda, please go the nurses' station, and a staff member will get it for you." I would catch hell as soon as the patients came into the lounge. My behavior had changed a simple soda bottle into a "sharp." We had so few privileges. Symbols of freedom and independence translated into personal dignity. I would pay for what I'd done, and the price would not be cheap. Although I had managed to salvage most of my privileges, I had cost the entire ward a significant one.

I waited in the lounge to get it over with. Sure enough, George dragged into the lounge for coffee. "What's this?" he said. "Who moved the sodas? What's with this sign?"

I looked up from where I was seated in front of a half-finished puzzle.

"Tyra, do you know . . . Hey, what's happened to your arm?" He pointed at it. "Why is it bandaged up to your elbow?"

"It's because of me, George. I cut my wrist with a Tab bottle last night. I'm really sorry about the sodas being moved. I didn't mean it." I teared up.

"Well that's just great. Poor Miss Tyra got sad and lost it. Now the rest of us can't get a soda without having to ask," he huffed.

"I'm real sorry, George. Really I am."

"All right then," George grumbled. "Every time I want a soda, I'm coming to you. The least you can do is get it for me from the nurses' station. I'm not the only one who'll be pissed. You know that, don't you?"

Sure enough, I was taunted and isolated for a few days. We all had the opportunity to "work on our anger," as the staff would say. I felt humiliated that my fellow patients had lost privileges because of me, but I soon grew tired of their insults, although I knew I deserved them.

Most importantly, I turned a corner. I began to think I could trust myself to recover. Dr. Roberts's belief in me meant everything. It gave me a monumental sense of hope. Even if I lost my privileges, I could get through it.

FOURTEEN

Girls Like You

Dr. Roberts prevailed. I didn't lose my group privileges and wasn't placed on watch. Mrs. Locke told me he had taken serious criticism from some of the hospital staff for letting me remain on group status. Except for Larry and my grandmother Nennie, both of whom were miles away, it had been years since I'd felt someone was in my corner. I rose to the occasion, determined not to let Dr. Roberts down.

I enjoyed the ritual of attending daily classes, especially art and piano once a week, and I looked forward to gym with most of the weller-than-well group, which Dr. Roberts said I needed to attend twice a day to help get me out of my head. I also enjoyed chatting with Forbes and my conversations with Mrs. Locke in the patient lounge at lunch and dinner. I became a fan of Kansas University basketball. It was the only thing I watched in the TV lounge. I'd loved basketball since Daddy took us to Austin when our hometown boys went to the high school state finals. Making egg salad for Trudi and playing the piano so George could sing "The Old Lamplighter" made me feel useful. I loved these people. They were my family now—unpretentious, sometimes unusual, but always interesting.

Deborah and I crossed paths in the hallway one day after my cutting episode. "How're you doing?" she asked. "I've wondered about you since you cut your wrist."

"I'm feeling better. Kind of like I turned a corner," I told her. "That cutting episode scared the crap out of me. It made me realize I better get this right, especially if I want approval to meet Larry for R&R."

"That's right," she exclaimed. "Yeah, you do need to clean your slate if you wanna go to Hawaii." She grinned. "Feel like company for a while?"

"Sure, let's grab a soda and go to my room." I was relieved to have company.

We went to my room, where Deborah plopped down on the end of my bed. I sat in the only chair. "Why did you cut your wrist?" she asked.

"I used to binge and purge to make my anxiety go away," I explained. "Then one day, I took a razor blade and cut my wrist. I don't know where the idea came from. I didn't plan to cut myself. It was just automatic, like a compulsion. The calm lasted longer than with binging and purging, but it was messier. Cutting works better but it feels sicker." I frowned.

"I know what you mean about a compulsion to do something," Deborah said slowly. "Do you want to know one of the main reasons I'm here?"

"Only if you want me to know," I said.

"Most of the time, I do pretty well, but . . . you won't tell anyone, will you?" she asked hesitantly.

"If you tell me it's a secret, it's between the two of us," I promised.

"For some reason—I don't know why—whenever I see a bus or a truck coming down the road, I have a strong urge to jump in front of it." She seemed to be looking at me for assurance.

"All I can say, Deborah, is I don't ever want you to hurt yourself. Is there a pattern, something that's a trigger that makes you feel like jumping?"

Deborah shook her head. "That's as much as I want to say today. Maybe we can talk about this again, but no more today."

"No problem," I agreed.

"I've been fussing about a secret that's bothering me," I confided. Since my arrival at Menninger, I'd talked about missing Larry and losing Daddy, but I had kept one of the biggest experiences of my life to myself.

"I'm thinking this might not be such a good idea," I paused, suddenly unsure.

Deborah was silent for a moment before she responded. "First of all, we're used to spilling our guts around here, you know?" she said. "Like, 'tell me how you're feeling,' they always say. Or, 'how do you feel about that?' I get sick of it some days. Don't worry about it so much. You can tell me anything you want. We don't know any of the same people, so who am I going to tell? Besides, it feels like you want to talk about it," she counseled, like we were prone to do with each other on occasion.

"Okay, here goes," I began. "I was kind of a mess in high school. My grades were respectable my freshman year but dropped my sophomore year. I didn't care about being a leader anymore. I lost interest in my friends. Beer became my new best friend," I admitted.

"That's not a good sign," Deborah frowned.

"By the end of junior year, I was drinking alone. I failed most of my classes. Every chance I could, I drove to the drive-in liquor store at the New Mexico state line thirty miles away. I even kept the amount I drank a secret from the few friends I had left."

Deborah frowned. "Where'd your mother think you were going all those times you left the house?"

"I told her I was going to the library to study."

"She believed that?"

"I think she knew better, but she was tired of arguing with me. She wanted my grades to improve, so maybe she told herself I really was going to the library. Anyway, I'd pull my mother's car up to the drive-in window at the liquor store and scan the parking lot for the liquor patrol board. If it was all clear, I'd order one or two six packs of Coors."

"Oh my God, you were brazen. Did you drink all that?" Though astonished, Deborah was also mesmerized.

"Yep. I drank alone in Mother's car, parked next to a jack pump pumping crude to its own rhythm. I listened to KOMA Radio, Oklahoma City. I was lonely and missed Daddy. I used to look up at the stars, searching for a sign from Daddy or even God. I was depressed and losing my way, and I knew it.

"Deborah, I don't think I ever got over losing Daddy. Lots of days, I'd skip school and drive to the cemetery, sit on his stone bench and talk with him, sometimes out loud and sometimes in my head. I felt him close by."

"Tyra, what happened to you?" Deborah asked. "Why do you think you felt so bad and alone?"

"What happened?" I parroted. "I got pregnant in May of my junior year. I was sixteen."

"Oh no, are you serious? Where's the baby now?" Deborah asked. She looked stunned.

"Hang on, I'll get to that," I said. The more I told Deborah, the more comfortable I felt.

"Mother asked me if I had missed a period. I told her I didn't think so, but she insisted I see our family doctor. He called and told Mother the test was positive. I overheard them on the phone. After she hung up, Mother looked right through me and said, 'He says you're three months pregnant.' She asked who the father was, and I told her. We didn't discuss it again until I was seven months along."

Deborah's eyes widened.

"It was like those times when I looked her straight in the eye and told her I was headed to the library to study, when really I was going to buy beer. She'd act as if what I had told her was true. We both knew I was lying. How's that for crazy making?" I slapped my knee.

"We acted as if the pregnancy wasn't real. Keeping it secret mattered most. I knew I couldn't keep it a secret forever, but I needed time to figure out what I was going to do. It was up to me to decide; Mother wasn't going to help. I did confide in one close friend, and I told the father of the baby, but I promised him that I would take care of everything."

Deborah wiped her eyes. "You were either very brave or very stupid. Sometimes I think they're the same thing." She patted my arm. "So what did you do?"

"The summer after my junior year, we moved to Abilene, where Mother had a scholarship to start her master's degree at Abilene Christian College. No one else in my hometown knew about the pregnancy. I enrolled in classes at the university high school to make up the subjects I'd failed junior year. We rented a house close to the university, and Mother and I walked to classes. I was five months along, but you couldn't tell from the jeans and long shirts I wore."

"At least that was one good thing." Deborah seemed to understand.

"At night, I'd lay in bed watching my stomach move, even though I couldn't admit to myself that I was pregnant. My Daddy's only sister, Aunt Ruth, and her husband, Uncle Joe, lived on the other side of Abilene close to the Baptist university. We often had dinner with them on weekends. Uncle Joe was a Baptist minister in a small country church and a carpenter. I used to wonder why he didn't talk about the devil and hell, like our preacher at home.

I decided it was because he was more like Jesus. After all, he was a carpenter." I cocked an irreverent eyebrow and giggled.

"I only talked to Daddy about my situation. I tried to imagine what he would tell me. I knew I had to get a plan and admit to Mother I was pregnant only after I had a solution. We were Southern Baptist, so I made an appointment with the pastor of a Baptist church there, thinking he might help me. But when I explained my situation, he said, 'We don't have anything for girls like you.'

"Deborah, I'll never forget his answer. 'Girls like you' made it sound like I had leprosy or something. Even Jesus told the men ready to stone the woman caught in adultery to cast the first stone only if they'd never sinned. Jesus forgave the woman. Do you remember that, Deborah?" I asked. "It's in the New Testament."

"No, Tyra, I don't." She smiled. "I'm Jewish. Now go on."

"I told my aunt I was having sinus problems and asked her for the name of their family doctor. I told the doctor something must be terribly wrong with me. He would probably think I was pregnant, but that was impossible. After examining me, he told me I was almost seven months along and that I should go home and tell my mother."

Deborah leaned in, captivated.

"I explained to him that I couldn't do that. My mother was a widow, and we lived in a small town where Mother was a teacher. I asked if he knew anyone who could help me. He said there was an adoption agency at the Church of Christ where he was a church leader. They could find me a place to live until the baby came, and the adoptive parents would pay my medical expenses. He asked if I would like to meet with a social worker there."

"Tyra, I am so glad someone came to your rescue," Deborah exclaimed. "That's amazing, don't you think? You just happen to pick the right doctor with connections to help you. Now go on. I want to hear the rest of it."

"Most of the time I lived in denial. But at night, when the baby moved, there was no denying it: I was pregnant. Keeping the baby was never an option. One thing I knew for sure was that my child would have a mother and a father. My baby would have a chance for a good education. There was no way I would deprive my child of that. The baby wouldn't pay for my stupidity. I loved my baby." My voice broke. Now that I was talking about it, all the anguish of that time six years ago was coming back.

Telling my secret about the baby to Deborah after all these years felt safe. Deborah had become a friend. Trust grew quickly between patients since we lived together. Even when I cut my wrist and the coke bottles had to be locked up, the other patients gave me a hard time, but they hadn't ostracized me.

"Are you getting tired of this?" I asked Deborah.

"Absolutely not! You can't stop now. I want to hear the ending." She sounded sincere.

"I met with the social worker at the church adoption agency and the woman who let 'girls like me' live with her until their babies were born. Her name was Ollie. She worked at the church, and her house was only two blocks away. Once I had everything worked out, I went home and told Mother I knew I was pregnant and that I had a plan. I asked her if she'd meet with me and the social worker, and she agreed."

Deborah nodded and gestured for me to keep going.

"We told no one except my aunt and uncle and my grand-mother Nennie. She offered to pay tuition for a high school tutor, so I could take courses through one of the local high schools. I'd have credits to transfer if I decided to go back home after the baby came," I explained.

"Nennie came to visit me often during my pregnancy and afterward. She and Ollie became good friends and didn't even argue over what Baptists believed about how you got to heaven versus what the Church of Christ believed.

"Ollie invited me to join her for TV in her part of the house, and we started cooking and eating our meals together, not like the other 'girls like me.' I was different from them. Anyway, that's what Ollie said." I shrugged, and Deborah nodded.

"Ollie treated you like family. That's so cool. It tickles me that Ollie wanted you." Deborah smiled.

"My baby girl was born in early October. I woke up one morning after Ollie had gone to work. My vision was blurry. It felt like someone had poured Karo syrup over my eyes. I could see the outlines of things, and color, but that was all. I had to fumble around for the muumuu I kept in the closet. Luckily, I remembered the social worker's number and managed to call it on the first try, counting the holes on the dial since my vision was too blurry to see. When his secretary answered, I said, 'Stephanie, this is Tyra. I'm not feeling so good.'

"'Mr. Macon's in a meeting,' she told me. 'Why don't you walk on over? That way, you'll be here when he gets out, and the two of you can decide if you need to see the doctor or if you feel up to keeping your appointment with your tutor.'

"I was really scared, but I acted calm. I didn't know if I could see well enough to walk the two blocks to the church, but I said, 'Sure, I can do that.'"

"Why didn't you just tell her what was going on?" Deborah looked incredulous.

"I didn't want to cause a problem. I felt so guilty that I tried not to be a burden."

"My God," Deborah sputtered with indignation.

"I headed for the church. I could hear cars stop and go at the traffic light and thanked God I didn't have to cross the main street, only the side one. I stood on the curb, listening and talking calmly to myself, but at the same time, I tried to hurry. I kept telling myself I could make it. It worked. I opened Mr. Macon's door and heard Stephanie say, 'How are you feeling now?'

"I told her I still couldn't see very well and that it was getting worse. Then I passed out." Deborah gasped.

"They told me after the baby was born that I had gone into convulsions and they'd had to call an ambulance. I had eclampsia. All I remembered later was being rolled on a gurney into the delivery room. A kind, red-haired nurse kept asking me how I was doing and telling me I would be fine.

"Deborah, even in the delivery room, I felt guilty. I finally told the nurse I was okay, but I asked her, 'Why are you being so kind to me? Don't you know I'm not married?'

"Mother and I had agreed that she wouldn't come when the baby was born," I went on. "She was a teacher and thought it would draw suspicion if she took time off work without a good reason."

"You must be kidding!" Deborah was so beside herself she jumped up off the bed.

I held up a hand, interrupting her. "Once I went into convulsions, the social worker called and told Mother she needed to come. Mother went to the nursery to see the baby first. She told me the baby was healthy and would be okay.

"She went back home the same day." My voice trailed off, as I recalled Mother leaving. Teary eyed, I said, "I knew better than to ask, but I really wanted her to stay."

FIFTEEN

Engagement and Wedding

Not long after I shared secrets with Deborah, the two of us got together one night before dinner with a new patient, Penny. The mother of four children, Penny was attractive and instantly popular. She always had the newest record albums. One had to have "credentials," or a psychiatric diagnosis, to be admitted to Menninger. But Penny's youthful style and perennially happy disposition made me wonder if she was just there for a break from her famous musician husband and all the responsibilities of living in the public spotlight. Certainly, she would soon be part of the weller-than-well group.

The three of us gathered in the lounge. I mentioned feeling disappointed that I had not received a letter from Larry lately.

"Tell us about your engagement and your wedding," Penny chirped. "That'll make you feel better, right?" Penny looked over at Deborah, who nodded.

For a minute, I was afraid Deborah might say something about our earlier talk. Instead, she said, "Talk about something wonderful with you and Larry."

I couldn't help but smile. Larry and I had made so many memories during our brief time together. Recalling them helped keep me going, and I was glad Deborah and Penny wanted to hear about Larry and me. I briefly described our first date and then launched into the story of our engagement and wedding. "Three months after we met, we were already acting like a married couple. There had been no official proposal, but it was an unspoken understanding between us. Still, I longed for the formal question," I admitted.

"Wow, you guys didn't waste any time!" Penny exclaimed. "What was your hurry?"

I shrugged. "It felt right—like we belonged together, not like we were rushing."

"One Sunday night before spring registration we were poring over the class schedule at Pop's, our favorite diner. Pop came out, grinning as he placed a warmed brownie à la mode topped with an unlit gold candle in front of me. Larry acted like he was surprised, but I could tell he was pretending."

"Was it a ring? In the brownie?" Penny's eyes shone with eagerness.

I shook my head no.

"Let her tell it," Deborah chimed in.

"Larry took my hand in his." I drew out the story, savoring the retelling. "Our knees pressed together under the table. He told me how much he loved me. 'Will you marry me?' he asked softly. 'Yes,' I said, before he could finish the question."

Deborah and Penny sighed in unison.

"Larry lit the candle and lifted me from my chair in a bear hug. We set the date for as soon as the spring semester ended. I was nineteen and Larry was twenty."

When I told the girls about our engagement, I left out the most important thing: When Larry took me home that night, I told him about the baby girl I'd given up for adoption just two years earlier. "Maybe you don't want to marry me now," I whispered after I confessed.

Tears filled his eyes as he pulled me to his chest. "Tyra, my daddy adopted me when he married my mother. I was three years old. If it hadn't been for him, I would be working in the lumber mills in Alabama. I love you. Maybe I love you even more now."

That was the moment I knew I belonged with Larry Hull forever.

"Nennie invited us to join her at Furr's Cafeteria in Lubbock for lunch not long after Larry's official proposal. She was the first person in my family we told about our engagement.

"'Have you picked out rings?' she asked. Embarrassed, Larry explained he was saving his money.

"Nennie told us about her friend and business associate who owned Connor Jewelry in Brownfield. Nennie had redecorated his store not long before and offered to speak with him. Mr. Connor gave clients the option of purchasing on credit. Our arrangements with him would be confidential."

"It sounds like your grandmother really was on your side," Deborah observed.

"She was always there for me," I acknowledged.

"A few weeks later, Larry and I went shopping for rings. Were we interested in plain bands or diamonds, Mr. Connor wanted to know. He pulled several sets from his glistening showcases and told us to take our time.

"Larry's eyes glistened as we took turns trying on rings. One set caught our attention, but it had no engagement ring. Larry was set on me having an engagement ring." All three of us girls smiled at that. "He asked Mr. Connor about solitaires. Mr. Connor left for a few minutes then came back with a sterling silver set. It had one small solitaire diamond ring and a wedding band with three tiny matching diamond chips on each side. The band for Larry matched mine.

"The set cost more than we'd planned to spend, but as soon as Mr. Connor opened the box, the look on Larry's face said it all."

The girls nodded, looking pleased.

"The engagement ring fit my finger like it was made for me. We agreed I would wear it out of the store. Then Larry met with Mr. Connor privately in his office. After a little while, he came out grinning."

"He's a persistent guy, that Larry," Deborah announced, as if she knew him personally.

"You're right. He never gives up," I agreed.

"That's what you need to remember when you get worried about him, Tyra," Deborah assured me, as if she had read my mind. "He's not a quitter. He'll be back from Vietnam."

"Go on with the wedding story," Penny urged.

"We joined my family for a celebratory lunch at my aunt's and uncle's. Everyone oohed and aahed over my ring," I continued, "except for my mom." My joy at the memory of that day dimmed a little.

Deborah scowled but kept quiet. After hearing about my pregnancy, she didn't have much patience for Mother.

"Larry and I invited Mother to join us for coffee before we left for home. She sat in the restaurant real quiet, almost sullen. Finally, she turned and spoke to Larry as if I wasn't sitting right there at the table." Deborah scowled harder. "She asked him how he was going to support me. Larry tried to reassure her. He promised we would both graduate from college. 'Mrs. Decker, we'll get by,' he told her.

"Mother forgot her manners. 'I didn't raise Tyra to just 'get by,' she said. 'She deserves better.'"

Penny gasped.

"I was so embarrassed at Mother's rudeness I could barely look up from my coffee. Larry sat tall in his chair. 'Mrs. Decker, I love your daughter,' he told her. 'I'll always care for her. We have dreams and promises to one another that we'll keep. I'll always love her, and she feels the same about me. I'm committed to changing your mind about me and our marriage.'"

"I love this guy!" Deborah exclaimed. "How cool is he?"

"I'd say he's pretty mature and confident. Some guys would have lost their tempers. He does sound special, Tyra," Penny agreed.

"Room for one more?" Mrs. Locke stepped into the lounge and pulled up a chair.

"Time for your shift already?" I asked as she sat down. "I'm talking about my engagement and wedding."

"Mrs. Locke, this is a good one," Deborah said.

"Keep going." Penny was anxious for me to continue.

Mrs. Locke nodded, so I went on. "Mother had been crazy about Daddy, so I didn't understand how she couldn't want the same for me. On the other hand, I was just nineteen and Larry only twenty," I defended Mother. "Given that Daddy had died, and that she hadn't finished college, she had good reason to worry that I might not complete school."

"You're too forgiving," Deborah said darkly. "Deep down, weren't you just a little mad?"

"I thought Mother acted selfish and impolite," I replied. "I understood her feelings, but I was going to marry Larry no matter what. He was my dream come true," I finished honestly. "Larry encouraged me to give Mother time, to try and understand that she just wanted the best for me. His confidence in standing up to my mother on our behalf without one shred of rudeness amazed me. He was my hero that day. He always will be."

"Your Larry has class. I know many people who don't come close to that kind of maturity," Mrs. Locke observed. I felt pleased that she recognized Larry's graciousness, too.

"Six months later, Mother told Larry how wrong she had been about him. She said he was a son-in-law who would make any mother-in-law proud. When Mother apologized, Larry hugged her and said, 'Mrs. Decker, you were only wanting the best for Tyra. I love being a part of this family.' Mother's eyes filled with tears and so did mine," I reminisced.

"Tell us the rest!" Penny insisted. "You can't skip over the wedding!"

We all laughed at her excitement. "We didn't have much time to prepare," I said. "We were both in school, and we were taking a course called 'Preparation for Marriage,' so we were really busy. Plus, we didn't have a whole lot of money. We were saving for after we were married, when we'd have to pay for our tuition and all our living expenses. There just wasn't any money for invitations, flowers, or a dress. Mother hadn't offered, and we weren't about to ask for help."

This time, Penny scowled along with Deborah.

"But a few months before the wedding, Nennie came to town on a mission. She wanted to make sure I had something nice for my big day."

Penny's face lit up.

"I was so grateful I was wearing a dress instead of jeans when we pulled up in front of Margaret's. It was the most sophisticated dress shop in Lubbock."

Penny clapped her hands in delight.

"Nennie asked Inez, her favorite saleslady, if they still had the beautiful mantilla veil she had admired at Christmastime. Inez brought the mantilla from the back of the store and steered me toward the three-way mirror. She arranged it on my head. It was exquisite. I remember thinking that while Daddy might have agreed with Mother that I was too young to be married, he would have approved of the veil. Like Nennie, Daddy loved beautiful things." Tears filled my eyes and even Mrs. Locke nodded appreciatively.

"'Wrap it up, Inez,' I heard my grandmother say. 'This is Tyra's first purchase for her wedding.'"

"I love mantillas," Penny exclaimed. "Nennie was your angel, wasn't she?"

"That's what grandmothers are for," Mrs. Locke chimed in.

"We chose May 28, 1966, to get married, even though Larry's dad was on temporary duty in Guam. Larry's mother was elated. That was a relief," I sighed. "Mother and my brother, Rodney, acted angry. I was never sure why. . . . I think they were afraid I wouldn't finish college. Mother finally agreed to go with me to pick out patterns for a wedding dress and a going-away suit for the honeymoon. She was a great seamstress, and it thrilled me when she found a gorgeous piece of wide lace to go down the front of my A-line wedding dress. It was simple and plain, a style I loved. And the lace didn't detract from the mantilla."

"Did the two of you have a good time shopping?" Penny asked, savoring every detail.

"Yes, we did. Mother was fantastic. She even paid for invitations and flowers. She took pride in her work; she couldn't help herself. Once she came to grips with the fact that Larry and I were determined to get married and weren't going to change our minds, she wanted me to look beautiful."

"That must have been comforting," Mrs. Locke acknowledged.

"For my going-away suit, we chose yellow linen. Linen is a favorite of mine. Larry and I had already decided we wanted to use daisies since they would be beautiful, in season, and inexpensive. Yellow and white were the colors of the day." I grinned.

"We ordered the invitations that weekend, selected the flowers, and booked the First Baptist church." Deborah rolled her eyes. "It was the church I grew up in and where we'd had Daddy's funeral.

"On his way to the rehearsal dinner, Larry's '57 Chevy broke down. He rode the rest of the way with Marty, his best man. After dinner, we asked Mother if we could take over the payments on my Corvair Monza. Thankfully, she said yes, with no admonitions like, 'I told you so.' Her wedding gift was to pay my college tuition until I graduated. We were thrilled."

"Who walked you down the aisle in place of your father?" Mrs. Locke asked.

"My brother, even though he agreed with Mother that I shouldn't be getting married. I think he felt burdened after Daddy died—like he had to become the man of the family then even though he was only a teenager.

"Our reception was in the fellowship hall at the church. We served wedding cake, mixed nuts, punch, and coffee. We had only the money Larry had saved from his part-time job."

"Where did you honeymoon?" Penny looked impatient to get to the most romantic part.

"Ruidoso, New Mexico. We went to a resort with a ski lift. We spent Saturday night on the road, Sunday night at the resort, and Monday night in Roswell with Larry's mother and little brother."

"A ski lift in May?" Deborah couldn't help herself.

"We didn't have much money. The resort was in the mountains. When we rode the gondola on Monday before we left, the scenery was beautiful. It was a quick trip but we needed to get back home. Neither of us had a job. That was next on our list. Even I thought it was kind of crazy that we had no work plans, but we believed it would work out," I finished.

"The wonder of young love," Mrs. Locke said, smiling.

"A week after the wedding, Mother moved three hundred miles away to Denton, Texas, to begin a new master's degree in Library Science. She was a teacher but wanted to be a school librarian. I was homesick for her; worried I'd never see her again. It was kind of like after Daddy died. I didn't want to leave Larry, but when

Mother left the wedding still upset with me about our marriage, I worried that if something happened to her my last times with her would have been when she was unhappy with me.

"Larry and Nennie took me to go see Mother on a weekend, but they had to get back for work on Monday. I stayed with Mother for several weeks, until she had time to take me home. I'll never forget when I knocked on the door to our apartment and Larry answered, I asked him, 'Can I come home?'

"He grabbed me in a tight hug. 'I'm so happy you're back,' he whispered in my ear.

"'But Larry, I can't cook.' I whined.

"'Don't worry, Tyra,' he assured me. 'I'll teach you.'"

SIXTEEN

~~~~~~~~

We Regret to Inform You

Menninger had become my home away from home. I felt safe and treasured my daily conversations with Dr. Roberts. I began to feel gratitude for the opportunities, people, and things that were good in my life. More and more often, hope overshadowed despair and sadness. I was no longer acting on my compulsions and earned individual privileges. I could walk on the grounds alone and go to the dining room and sit with whom I pleased. These small things felt monumental.

I saw Menninger as an opportunity to start anew. I couldn't wait until I met Larry for R&R, and for the time he and Laura and I could be together again. I still obsessed about his safety, but I learned through my work with Dr. Roberts that some of that was realistic—Larry was at war—and some of it was that old obsession of losing those I loved, as if it were preordained.

On February 21, 1971, I waited in my room for my standing 3:00 coffee and walk with Dr. Roberts.

"We're not going for coffee today," he said when I answered his knock on my door. "We'll talk here."

"What's wrong?" I demanded, certain that I already knew. A voice in my head screamed, *Larry is dead!*

Dr. Roberts closed the door behind him and pulled up the desk chair. "Mrs. Hull, your husband has been killed." His voice wavered as he struggled to maintain a professional demeanor. Sadness filled his eyes. "His plane crashed."

Time moved as if in slow motion. Larry's loveable grin flashed before me. *No, no, don't leave. Don't go. Please don't.* I pleaded with him in my head as I slumped onto the bed. I curled my knees to my chest and wrapped my arms around them tight.

Dr. Roberts sat silently for a few minutes as a parade of all the souls I had lost marched through my mind, led by Daddy. Larry brought up the rear.

"Mrs. Hull?" Dr. Roberts leaned nearer to me. "They believe he was killed instantly."

"He's dead like my daddy is dead." My voice sounded wooden.

"Yes, he's dead. Yes, your father died when you were a child." Dr. Roberts spoke slowly. I could still see my father lying in his casket in the funeral home parlor. At the visitation, I had moved a chair over, climbed up on it, and kissed him good-bye.

At least Dr. Roberts was saying the words, not like when Daddy died and no one would speak the truth. "Your husband has been killed in Vietnam," Dr. Roberts said again. "I don't know any more of the details, but when you feel ready, officers from Forbes Air Force Base will deliver the official letter."

Dr. Roberts left to go on rounds, assuring me that he'd stop by again before he left the ward. I forced myself to stay in the present. I was at Menninger. Larry was dead. Laura had just lost her daddy. With that, reality set in, along with a powerful longing. I would have given anything to talk to my husband right then.

I walked down the hall to the pay phone. I couldn't speak with Larry, but I could call my mother. The ward hummed with activity. Bits of conversations and music from a record player floated through the door of the patient lounge. From the TV room, I could hear the weatherman predicting snow. Dr. Roberts must have spoken to the staff about Larry; the nurse didn't question me when I asked to use the pay phone. She moved from the nurses' station out into the hall, expressed her condolences, and unlocked the booth.

I shivered as I stepped inside and dialed our house in West Texas. I got no answer. I could see the clock on the wall: 5:30 p.m. I placed the receiver back in its cradle and contemplated. My mother was a librarian at the elementary school. Work was over by now. Where would she be this time of day?

I called Josephine, my mother's friend, at her restaurant. Mother often dropped by there for coffee after work.

"What's wrong?" Josephine sounded surprised to hear my voice. "Your mother's not here. I haven't seen her today. Are you all right?"

Ignoring her questions I said, "I need to reach Mother. If you talk to her, please tell her to call me."

"Are you sure you're all right?" Josephine pressed.

"Of course I'm all right," I snapped. "I'm in a hospital. Please, just have Mother call me."

I felt bad after I hung up. Mom and Josephine had been friends since I was two years old, and I felt guilty for being so curt with her.

I thought about Laura as I made my way back to my room. I wasn't even sure she remembered her daddy or me anymore. I knew all too well the devastation of losing a parent. I wasn't about to let my daughter grow up an orphan. I had to get well now, so I could take care of my baby.

Later that evening, one of the nurses stuck her head in my room and whispered, "You have a call."

As I walked to the pay phone, I rehearsed what I'd say to Mother. I straightened my back and held my chin high, like I had seen her do when Daddy died. The receiver was lying on the small shelf inside the booth. I stared at it, postponing the inevitable, then finally snatched it up and held it to my ear. "Mom, it's me, Tyra. Mom . . ."

I couldn't get the words "Larry is dead" out. I sat on the bench, sobbing. Some younger part of me, my nine-year-old self, stepped in admonishing, *Straighten Up. Act right. You were going to say the words. Say the words!*

"Mother, Larry is dead," I choked out. "His plane crashed. They think he was shot down." I was too numb with shock to fully comprehend the words even as they tumbled out of my mouth.

"I was afraid of that." Mother's voice was filled with sorrow. "Josephine called around town looking for me. I went to the pharmacy to pick up a prescription, and the first thing the pharmacist said was, 'You need to call your daughter in Kansas.'" Mother's voice broke.

"Honey, I'm so sorry." I knew she meant it. Larry had won her over, though she hadn't made it easy for him at the start. She'd been so proud of him that when he'd graduated from Texas Tech, she'd bought him his first suit for graduation.

I wanted to whine about how unfair it felt, losing Daddy and now Larry. But I didn't dare. This was Mother, who knew even more about loss than I did. I longed to go home so she could comfort me, but Menninger was where I needed to be right now. Before arriving at the Clinic, I hadn't been able to stop cutting or binging and purging for any extended period of time. Here, I had gotten control of both. I hadn't cut myself since the incident with the soda bottle, and except for occasional slips with food, I'd done really well coping with my feelings. It was a good thing I was still here now. I had lost Larry, but Dr. Roberts and the staff would help me get through this.

I tried to reassure Mother over the phone that despite this most recent tragedy, I was all right. We both stifled tears, but our quivering voices betrayed us as we said good-bye.

I walked back to my room. I caught a glimpse of Becky in the shadows of her room next to the nurses' station, looking like Boo Radley in *To Kill a Mockingbird.* I often wondered if she was our own Boo, painfully shy but with the heart of a heroine. I passed a few other patients and staffers, avoiding eye contact with everyone.

Larry wasn't coming back. *Ever.* The reality struck hard: Larry wasn't just gone; he was *dead.* I argued with the truth like I had when Daddy died. I'd begged God for the chance to do it over. I'd promised if we got another chance to keep Daddy, I would never cry or be homesick again when he and Mother left looking for a cure.

What would I do without Larry? Panic swept over me. He had steadied me, made me believe that I was strong. Fear overcame me quickly, and I gasped. Then came another awful thought: What if the air force wouldn't pay for my treatment anymore? How could I ever take care of Laura if I couldn't get well? Overwhelmed, I closed my eyes. I could see Larry so clearly in my imagination. But I could never take care of Laura and myself if I walked through life with my eyes closed, trying desperately to conjure my dead husband every time I was frightened. I opened my eyes again, determined to face whatever came next.

After he left for Southeast Asia, Larry and I had mailed each other cassette tapes as well as letters. I treasured his tapes, though his voice was stilted, with long pauses between sentences. I didn't care; those tapes held his essence. They carried him back to me across the vast gulf that separated us. I grabbed a tape now, seeking something to quell the panic rising inside me. I put it in the cassette player and closed my eyes. At the sound of Larry's voice, I could practically see and feel him. He said, "Do what the doctors tell you, girl. Stick in there. Get well and get that degree." I heard planes taking off and landing in the background. "I want you to get it for you, not for me," Larry urged. "Don't forget, you're going to be a teacher." His voice was soft and reassuring. "We can do anything we set our minds to. You can do this. I'll see you soon."

The tape was also filled with talk about our trip to Hawaii for R&R. We had been planning it since before Larry left for Vietnam, counting the days until we could go. This cassette was a one-sided discussion about where we might stay and what we might do there. Larry used significant tape time critiquing various hotels and cottages some of the men in his unit had rented while they were on leave. In a way, through our exchange of tapes, we had traveled numerous times to Hawaii since Larry had shipped out. I realized with relief that in my mind's eye I could see the trip we'd been planning even though we would never take it. I could still go there in my imagination whenever I felt like it.

The epitaph, *To live in hearts we leave behind is not to die,* rang in my head. It was a line from a poem by Thomas Campbell engraved on the bench at Daddy's grave. A strange sense of comfort embraced me. In my mind, I'd been traveling to Hawaii to meet Larry whenever I missed him. Each time, he walked up the beach to meet me; he took my hand as we walked barefoot where the water and sand met. I could still meet him there whenever I longed for him, whenever I needed advice about Laura, whenever I wanted to give up.

On that day I made Larry a promise: I would always meet him where the water meets the sand. Forget 'til death do us part. Our devotion to one another was stronger.

~~~~~~~~

SEVENTEEN

Be with Us

Later that evening, a loud knock on my door startled me. When I opened it, I was stunned to see all five feet eleven inches of Emily, the patient I'd met in the lounge the day I arrived, towering over me. Emily lived in a spaceship and traveled to faraway places. On two previous occasions, she had invited me to travel with her. I had been flattered that she trusted me enough to ask me along but had felt fearful about playing make-believe with her. For Emily, her outer space world was real. In space, she was protected from the fears, hurts, and abandonments the rest of us experienced on Earth. I feared that if I traveled with her, I might find her fantasy world too enticing and be unable to find my way back to reality.

I'm five feet five inches tall. It was typical for Emily to stare, trancelike, way above my head. But tonight, her blue eyes met my own. Missing was the clump of yarn tangled between two knitting needles she usually carried around. Instead, her long arms hung limply at her sides, her only movement the compulsive pressing of her fingers to the thumb on each hand.

"Tyra, I am sorry to hear about your husband's death." A tortuous silence passed. Emily rocked back and forth in her Scandinavian clogs. Her lucidity caught me by surprise. Fearing I might say the wrong thing, I kept quiet.

"I said, I'm sorry about the death of your husband in Vietnam today." She repeated herself, as if I hadn't heard her. Tears filled my eyes. Emily's pain and fear of reality were real, and I knew it.

Yet she had come back from her spaceship to comfort me. Compassion engulfed me, but I had no words for Emily. Sobs erupted from my throat.

Still staring into my eyes, she said, "You know I have to go. Come with me. You can come with me."

I was so tempted to leave my pain behind and travel with her that it forced hateful words out of my mouth: "Your spaceship's not real!"

Hurt and anger clouded Emily's face. Her eyes shifted to their usual place above my head. "I have to go," she mumbled. She turned her huge frame around, then shuffled robotically down the hall.

Emily's compassion for me had been stronger than her fear of reality. The courage it took for her to come to my room and look into my eyes was hard for me to fathom. It was enormous; I was sure of that. *If you step on a crack, you break your mother's back.* The old childhood chant echoed through my throbbing head. Had I broken Emily's spirit? How could I have been so cruel? She had come to comfort me, and I had scared her back into outer space. Shit. I was just plain shit.

Soon there was another knock on the door. It cracked open a few inches. "Tyra, I'm coming in, okay? Tyra, I'm coming in. It's Penny."

She stepped into my room and without waiting for permission, Penny continued, "I've got a brand new record. Everyone's down in the patient lounge. Everyone's there. We want you to come down. Tyra, come be with us. Be with people. Everyone wants you to come. Don't be alone in your room. See my new record? Look, it's this new guy, James Taylor. It's called *Sweet Baby James*."

"Just give me a few minutes," I replied, intent on acting right this time. "You go on back and tell them I'm coming. I need to wash my face."

As Penny left, she touched my shoulder. "I'm so sorry," she said.

When I got to the patient lounge, every seat was occupied except for the large lumpy armchair upholstered in rust and chocolate brown tweed, which sat empty against the wall across from the three-seat sofa. As I stepped into the lounge, Penny met me at the door. She took my hand and led me to my seat of honor.

"See, we're all here," she gently coaxed.

I had hardly sat down when George thrust a Styrofoam cup of coffee into my hand. "I'm not sure it's mixed right. I wasn't sure how much coffee, how much water. It has sugar and that white powdered cream stuff. Water's not too hot . . . hope it's okay."

"George, it's fine. Really, it is," I assured him, scooting deeper into the soft cushioned seat. I loved these people. They were family now. I leaned my shoulders against the chair back and gazed over the crowd. George sat to my left. The weller-than-well group—Forbes, Deborah, and Lainey—turned their sorrowful eyes toward me like three wise guardians of some semblance of sanity. I wondered whether I'd fit in the weller-than-well group now that Larry was dead. I didn't want to lose all the progress I had made in the nearly five months I'd been at Menninger, and I vowed to do my best to stay in a good place emotionally.

We would not play the piano and sing "The Old Lamplighter" tonight, like we usually did.

The minister's wife knitted in the rocking chair on the far side of the room next to the kitchenette. Cassandra sat across the room in her usual cross-legged pose on the floor in front of the love seat, rocking her body back and forth and muttering, "Jesus in my mind's eye, Jesus in my mind's eye." Skylar sat near Cassandra. Her blond hair was combed, and bright red lipstick outlined the place she thought her mouth belonged. Her painted cherry red lips plunged downward into a frown, a testament to her ability to comprehend the sadness of the occasion.

I caught a glimpse of my nine-year-old self in the far corner of the room, bare feet dangling off the piano bench. She was my secret confidant, wise and sure of herself. Her petite frame, adorned with blond pigtails, sat erect and invisible to everyone but me. I called her "T," short for T-Texas Tyra—the nickname my Uncle Leonard had given me when I was little.

Our blue eyes met across the room. *We've been in a group like this before,* T said. *Remember when Daddy died and the minister came with all those church people?*

There's no minister tonight, but we've got a minister's wife, I acknowledged silently to my younger self.

T agreed. *I like her better. She doesn't act like she's the boss of everybody. Why did he act like he was the boss when Daddy died? Daddy was dead! No one was in charge!*

I heard her loud and clear in my mind and responded in kind. *Larry is dead. No one's in charge.*

Yep, this time we know what's coming, she said.

I offered my consensus: *Larry is dead. No one here pretends to know anything. No one's in charge. We're just here. Together. Nothing to be done. Sorry. We're so sorry. Nothing but sorry. Sad. Just sad. That's okay. No need to say anything.* I trusted the intentions of this group of mourners more than I had trusted those bearing sympathy when my daddy died in 1956.

Arms crossed in front of her chest, blue-eyed T confronted me. *You know Larry's dead like Daddy was dead.*

Larry is dead like Daddy is dead, I confirmed.

Both dead, we chimed in unison.

Daddy finally got sick enough to die.

Larry's plane finally crashed.

"You're supposed to have food." Skylar interrupted my silent conversation with my younger self. Clad in short shorts as short as the staff would allow and her skin-tight, white patent go-go boots, she narrowly avoided a mishap as she threw her long legs over Cassandra's head, then bounded over to the small refrigerator underneath the kitchenette counter.

"There's no good food," Skylar announced. Penny moved to the refrigerator to help soothe Skylar's preoccupation with offering edibles as tranquilizers. She convinced Skylar that moldy blueberry yogurt was not the thing to serve on this occasion. She said the group could invite me to join them in the dining room to have a meal in memory of my dead husband tomorrow.

Trudi walked in. "What, a party? Where should I sit? Whose party? Where's my seat? A birthday? Who invited me?"

Penny moved to Trudi's side. I heard her whisper, "Tyra's husband was killed."

"He's dead? Tyra's husband is dead? In the war? A party for Tyra's dead husband?" Trudi's shrill words pierced the room.

Penny told Trudi she was welcome to stay, but she'd have to lower her voice. Trudi shuffled over to me. "Egg salad." she demanded. "Where's my sandwich?"

Tonight, the night of Larry's death, the night a party was being held without her, Trudi wanted her egg salad sandwich as usual. A part of me wanted to give it to her. It was our nightly ritual before bedtime, a routine comfort.

But Penny insisted there would be no egg salad tonight.

"It's a hell of a country club," Trudi griped. "A hell of a hospital. No invitation for Trudi." She shuffled back out of the lounge.

Penny placed James Taylor's new album on the record player and eased into the chair next to me. Everyone quieted as Taylor's soothing voice wafted over the group. Cassandra's mantra softened until it was barely audible as she chanted, "Jesus in my mind's eye," to the beat of the music. A hypnotic fog settled over the group.

On the other side of the room, T's bare feet swung back and forth in time with the music. *This is better than before,* we both thought as our eyes met. It was as if this family knew how we felt and what we needed.

I loved it when Skylar tried to get us some food. She knows what you're supposed to do when someone dies, I chuckled to myself.

Remember when Daddy died and all those church people kept bringing all that food? T continued my train of thought.

And then Pa Decker died. And Uncle Frank died. And then PaPa died. I finished the memory.

The church people and relatives always brought food! Flowers and food! Why did they always bring the best food when someone died? Why do you think they saved the best food for then? T asked.

Why never the best roses until someone died? I threw back.

Our assessment of then and now was the same. The other patients' confusion and anxiety at this special gathering matched the commotion and chaos I'd felt when Daddy died.

Did you hear Trudi? T continued.

She felt so bad because she thought everyone but her got invited to the party for Larry. I felt sorry for her. Did you? I asked. *She knows the truth. No one remembers her 'cause they don't like her.*

Let me talk, T admonished. *I don't like her some days, either. But I loved her tonight when she yelled out 'cause she thought she wasn't invited! Did you see their faces? They got caught. She caught them having a party without her. Caught 'em red-handed!*

Seated in my appointed chair just as my mother had been to welcome those bearing sympathy when Daddy died, I smiled at T as she slipped off the piano bench and tiptoed barefoot across the room, unseen by the others. She approached the brown and rust chair, and I opened my arms and lifted her to my lap. I assured her I could and would bring home the bacon. I lacked one more year of college, then I'd become a teacher. She was not to worry; she could count on me to act like a grown-up and get well.

As she laid her pigtailed head against my bosom, we crossed over some sort of divide. We weren't running from or drowning in the pain. We were mourning Daddy and Larry, and all the losses we had endured over the years. The chaos in the room soothed us. It matched the chaos we felt.

James Taylor's "Fire and Rain" began to play. When James Taylor sang the part about sweet dreams and flying machines, George jumped to his feet. "Stop!" he screamed. "This is not good music! Get it off!"

Penny raced to the record player and removed the record as Skylar anxiously shook the leg she had draped over the arm of the couch. "Bad. It's bad," she declared.

My eyes met T's as she looked up from my lap. She reminded me of Laura. T smiled at me. *Daddy is dead. Larry is dead.*

EIGHTEEN

Memorial Service

Two days later, officers from Forbes Air Force Base hand-delivered the official letter informing me that Larry had been killed in action. I cried silently as I read the letter, which stated that he had been killed on February 19, 1971, when his plane went down in Southeast Asia. Due to hostile enemy fire, it wasn't possible to retrieve his remains. Distraught, I tried as hard as I could to maintain my composure. Although my emotional state was still very fragile, I was determined to represent Larry with dignity. I would be courageous and act right so Larry would be proud of me.

After Larry's death, I had new responsibilities. I had to step up—not succumb to my fears but push through them. I was solely responsible for Laura and myself now. I wondered what the officers thought about bringing the regret letter to the next of kin in a mental hospital. Years later, I discovered I was right to be concerned. While reading through Larry's complete file from the air force, I discovered a dialogue among authorities about whether Laura should stay with her caregivers since I was hospitalized, or be placed in the care of Larry's parents. Thank God my doctors at Menninger had advised that I would be able to take care of Laura again, and she should stay put until then.

That night my sleep was fraught with dreams of my promise to bury Larry at Arlington if he didn't survive. I awoke the next morning feeling anxious and burdened. The letter said his remains were unrecoverable due to heavy enemy fire. Did that mean his body would never come home? I couldn't bear that thought. Maybe it meant the enemy fire was too heavy and that after the battle moved on, they could retrieve him. But what if they couldn't? Should we have a memorial service now?

Mother, my brother Rodney, and his wife, Jeri, were on their way to Topeka, and Larry's parents were flying in from Guam. What should I do? Suddenly, I knew: I would call the colonel who had written the regret letter.

I was on a mission as I headed down the green-carpeted hall to the phone booth. Patient phone privileges were covered by special rules and regulations, but those didn't seem to apply to me anymore.

When I called the number on the letterhead, a secretary answered.

"Ma'am," I said, "my husband, Lt. James L. Hull, got shot down in Vietnam. His body hasn't been recovered due to heavy enemy fire. The regret letter says it's unknown when his remains will come home. Ma'am, I'm a patient at the Menninger Clinic in Topeka, Kansas. My husband's parents live on the air force base in Guam. All of my family is in Texas. I need to talk to the colonel about what to do next. I promised Larry he'd be buried at Arlington, so I don't want to have a memorial service if his remains are coming home. Ma'am, please, I need to ask the colonel whether I should have a memorial service now, or wait until Larry comes home."

My distressed explanation must have convinced her to put me through. I blurted my story out to the colonel in a similar rush, desperate to explain the overwhelmingly complicated circumstances.

His kindness was palpable. "Mrs. Hull, please accept my condolences. I recommend you have a memorial service for your husband now. Make it as much like a funeral as you can. We don't know when his remains will be returned, or if they'll be returned at all. Please accept my sincere condolences and pass them on to your family and Lt. Hull's family as well."

The colonel's suggestion made sense. He was a colonel in the air force. If he didn't know what to do, who would? I decided to take his advice.

I was nervous about returning to Seminole for Larry's memorial service, but it was the best place to hold it, since his parents didn't reside in the States and all of my family lived within one-hundred miles of my hometown. Everyone who mattered at home knew I had hospitalized myself, and I felt unsure about my ability to cope with the upcoming trip without resorting to binging and purging. I asked Dr. Roberts if Mrs. Locke could accompany me home. He gave his permission, and she agreed to the job. The additional gossip that Mrs. Locke's presence might fuel was not as great as my fear of falling apart once I left the Clinic and was back in the middle of family dynamics.

Larry had been killed on February 19, 1971. We scheduled the memorial service for the following week. My mother, brother, and sister-in-law drove back to Texas to begin making arrangements for the service, while Mrs. Locke, Mama and Papa Hull, and I flew to Lubbock.

The one bright spot in this terrible tragedy was that I would see Laura sooner than I had expected. I'd missed her terribly over the months I'd been at Menninger and longed to somehow make it up to her. Like me, Laura would grow up without a daddy. The difference was, she was so young she most likely wouldn't remember the blue-eyed, blond man who had adored her.

After landing in Lubbock, we walked through the same terminal where Larry had boarded the plane for Vietnam. As I stepped outside into the parking lot, I was struck with an overwhelming wave of dread and fear. It was the same dread I'd felt when Laura and I had said good-bye to Larry just eight months earlier. This was where the three of us had shared our last hug, with Laura sandwiched between Larry and me. It would always be the last place Larry kissed me. In some ways it felt like a lifetime had passed. In others, it seemed like it had been just yesterday.

As we drove to the Lamberts, I agonized over how Laura would act when she saw me. She wasn't even two years old, and I'd been hospitalized almost five months. Would she remember me? What if she didn't, and clung to Marjorie Lambert instead? Walking through the Lubbock airport hadn't been easy, but I had done it. I wasn't sure I could stand it if Laura didn't recognize me, though.

My brother pulled his car into the Lamberts' driveway. As soon as the car stopped moving, I bounded from the car to the front porch. The excitement I felt at the opportunity to take Laura in my arms was greater than my fear. The door opened and there she was, taller, with some of her baby fat gone, calling, "Mommy, Mommy!" I was thrilled by her reaction and overcome with gratitude. My daughter knew who I was. Pulling her into my arms, I hugged her tight. Someone had made sure she didn't forget me. I'm forever grateful to the Lamberts for that.

~~~

The ninety-minute drive to my mother's house sped by. The last time I'd been there I was a wreck, and for a moment I trembled, recalling how ill I'd been. I looked over at Mrs. Locke, and that helped me steady myself. I reminded myself that I was on the way to being weller than well; I was already well enough to organize and attend Larry's service. That calmed me. Throughout my time in Seminole, Larry's voice whispered in my ear, "It came to pass, Tyra. You don't have to worry about it anymore. It came to pass." At some point, those words morphed into, "It's over. It happened.

Don't forget. I'm here. Whenever you need me, meet me where the water meets the sand. I love you."

I promised myself and Larry that I wouldn't cry at his service. I would stand tall and proud. If anyone was inclined to think I was like the people at the insane asylum down the road in Big Spring, I would show them I was not.

The Solomons, friends who owned a motel, stopped by and dropped off complimentary room keys for loved ones and friends arriving for Larry's service. It was just one of the many generosities our friends and neighbors showed to our family that weekend. In addition to Larry's parents, Mama Hull's sister, Mabel, and her preacher husband, Norm, drove in from Mobile, Alabama. Larry and I had spent one night with them when he took me to meet his Alabama relatives. In my mind's eye, I whispered to Larry, *Remember when Uncle Norm took us crabbing off the pier in Mobile and you had to show me what to do? It was the first real vacation we had taken since we married. We were so excited because you had just graduated from Tech and we had just found out I was pregnant. All our dreams were coming true. We were so hopeful about our future.*

The colonel had advised that we make the service as much like a funeral as possible. I knew how to do funerals. Daddy's was my blueprint. As we completed the arrangements the next day, I struggled privately with one big question: If this was to be a funeral and Larry's body wasn't home, what would be the focal point in the front of the church where the casket normally sat? Mr. Frazier, the art teacher at the local high school, owned a flower shop. I borrowed Mother's car and drove alone to the florist's. I asked him to help me design a flower arrangement to go at the front of the church.

"Did you have anything in mind?" Mr. Frasier wanted to know.

It had to be red, white, and blue, in the shape of a cross.

"This arrangement will be beautiful. Just right for your Larry," Mr. Frasier assured me, as he described a large easel of red and blue carnations. "We'll wrap one lei of white roses around the center bar of the cross; one blue satin banner inscribed 'Lt. James L. Hull' will drape diagonally across the center of the arrangement; and we'll add another one with the words *US Air Force* in gold at the base of it. What do you think?" he asked.

I nodded, pleased. It wasn't the traditional open casket, but with a photo of Larry on an easel next to it, it was the best we could do.

When I returned to Mother's, Mrs. Locke was standing at the front door. "Would you like a break?" she asked. She had an uncanny way of knowing when I needed one. I followed her back to what had been my brother's bedroom before he'd left for college and lay down on the bed.

Being back in Seminole wasn't easy for me. Memories from my childhood haunted me, returning me to the day my father died and my childhood ended. A car had pulled into our driveway. Mr. Doncaster, Daddy's business manager, rushed through our garage and peered through the screen door at Mother, who was on her hands and knees scrubbing the kitchen floor. "Dorothy, you'd better come now," he insisted.

"As soon as I get this water cleaned up . . . and I'll need to change clothes," she replied.

"It's bad," he insisted louder. "You need to come now."

Mother adored Daddy. But it was not the first or second time Daddy had gone to the hospital, and they were a proud couple. She wouldn't have wanted to appear dirty and in cleaning clothes at the emergency room.

As I planned Larry's funeral, I understood something else: Mother must have kept scrubbing because her heart couldn't bear the thought of what waited for her at the hospital. She must have known fear and dread, too. How had she moved through it without falling apart? I couldn't. What was wrong with me?

On that awful day, we had driven to the hospital, and Mr. Doncaster pulled up to the emergency entrance.

"Stay in the car," Mother said to me, looking both determined and scared. I watched as she and Mr. Doncaster walked into the hospital.

As many times as we had gone to see Daddy in the hospital, we had never used the emergency door. I hunkered down on the floorboard behind the driver's seat. It was June and must have been a hundred degrees outside. I cried and sweated and prayed for what seemed like forever. I was frantic; terrified this was the day Daddy really was going to die. *Maybe he's dead already*, I whimpered silently.

Mr. Doncaster opened the driver's side door after what seemed like hours. "Tyra, are you in here?" he called. The back door opened, and I felt his hand on my shoulder. "Tyra, get up. I'm taking you home with me." He said nothing about Daddy or about where Mother was. I didn't ask. I knew. No one told me, but I knew. I was furious.

We stopped by the swimming pool to pick up his two children. When we went inside the fenced-in pool area, one of my best friends, Peggy, hollered hello to me. Mr. Palmer, the physical education teacher, was on lifeguard duty. He asked how I was doing, and I answered that I was fine. I couldn't understand how my whole world had been turned upside down, yet everyone else kept on swimming, like it was any other summer day. What was wrong with them? Didn't they know something terrible had just happened? Didn't they care?

When Mr. Doncaster's car turned the corner onto our street later that evening, cars were lined up on both sides of the block. Lots of church people were standing in our front yard. I walked up the drive feeling dazed by all the commotion. PaPa Sexton stood on the front steps. I ran to him and threw my arms around his waist. He hugged me tight against him and then told me to go on in the house and find my mother.

She was sitting in the living room. Our minister and Nennie were on the sofa across from her. Mother had changed clothes. Quiet tears ran down Mother's face. As I ran across the room to her, I began to sob. Mother held me and brushed the hair from my eyes as she always did. "I thought I would never see you again," I cried.

"Oh honey, I'm here. I'll always be," she whispered in my ear. But that wasn't true, no matter how much we both wanted to believe it. She and I would never be the same. No one had told me, but I knew. Daddy was gone.

Everything changed right then and there, as Mother, who was seven months pregnant, began to rely on me to help her. "Tyra, it's getting late, and your brother is still out riding Reno. Someone needs to go get him and tell him about Daddy. Will you be a big girl and go with Mrs. Scott and Mrs. Simpson, show them the way to the stables?"

I nodded, then slipped out of my mother's arms and turned to my grandmother. "Nennie, I love you." I crawled up in her lap and sobbed into her soft chest while she rocked me like a baby. "Now," she said a few minutes later, once my sobs had subsided, "go find your brother."

I sat in the back seat of Mrs. Simpson's car, listening as she and Mrs. Scott talked in whispered tones about how sad it all was. I wondered if they'd forgotten that I was there or thought I was deaf.

"Who's going to bring home the bacon now?" I blurted out.

Mrs. Scott turned in her seat, her chubby arm stretching into the back toward me. "You don't need to worry your head about things like that."

"Somebody better worry about it," I retorted hotly. "Somebody's got to. Daddy always brings home the bacon. Mother cooks it. That's what they always say. If Daddy's gone, Mother will have to bring it home."

When we arrived at the stables, Rodney stared at us, confused. "We came to take you home," Mrs. Simpson told him. "There's been an emergency."

Rodney looked at me and then at her. He didn't ask what the emergency was. We got back into the car, and I slammed my door. I wasn't talking to any of these people anymore. They didn't speak the truth. My brother was no better. He was a sissy. He should have asked, "What's the emergency?" Didn't he care?

When we got home, I went out back to sit on the swing. My friend, Teri, and her parents walked over from their house. Teri sat down in the empty swing seat next to me as her parents went inside. We dragged our feet back and forth in the red dirt below the swings.

"Teri, Daddy's dead. They took him to the emergency." There. I'd said it out loud. I was furious I had to be the first to say it.

"I know," Teri said. "My mother already told me. I'm not supposed to talk to you about it," she murmured.

"It's about time somebody said it," I whimpered. "Why don't grown-ups just say the words? 'Your daddy's dead, dead, dead.' Teri, why don't they just say the words?"

Later, after Teri went home, one of the church ladies came out and asked me if I wanted to get something to eat or go play with the other children. What was wrong with these people? Didn't they know my daddy had just died?

I wanted them all to go home.

It started to get dark and some of the visitors finally left. I went into the house. Mother was still sitting in the same chair. The living room was crowded with people.

"Mother, why don't these people go home and leave us alone?"

Horrified, Mother shushed me. "Tyra, honey, they're here to give their sympathies and to be with us. Would you like to take a bath and go to bed?"

I headed for my bedroom to get my pajamas. As I left the living room, one of the church ladies I didn't know asked me if I needed help.

"I'm nine years old. I can take care of myself," I snapped. The room went silent as sorrowful eyes turned and stared at me. As I stormed out, I declared with more bravado than I felt, "Somebody around here's gonna have to bring home the bacon."

~~~~~

I spent an hour or so in my brother's old room, recalling that awful day my father passed away. Eventually, I joined the crowd of church people, family, and friends gathered in our home to mourn Larry. I tried my best to stay out of the past and in the present. It all was so much like what had happened after Daddy died, and many of the faces were the same. As I stepped into the family room, I felt all eyes on me again. I wondered if they were thinking that I was crazy and couldn't be trusted to come to Larry's memorial service alone. I tried to remind myself that the people gathered around me meant well, except perhaps for a few who were probably there out of curiosity.

The day had been long, and I still had to get through dinner. I didn't consider binging or purging. It was out of the question. The purpose of my trip was to honor and celebrate Larry's life and to acknowledge our terrible loss. I was determined to behave with dignity and to act right so Larry would have been proud. The night I learned Larry was killed and T and I discussed the events of losing Larry and Daddy as we sat among my patient family in the lounge, something inside gave me strength. It was as if God gave me a chance to redo Daddy's death the way I thought it should have been done when I was nine years old. I'd turned a corner that night. I had to step up. Laura depended on me, and I had promised Larry I would take care of her.

I found Laura and pulled her onto my lap. She looked up at me with blue eyes the color of Larry's. I would get well. Laura would live with me again. We would start our lives over. Not in Texas but in Kansas, where I could still see my doctors. Where Larry had never lived. Maybe I wouldn't miss him so much in a place where we had never been together. I had promises to keep. I needed to finish school and become a teacher, so I could bring home the bacon. And someday, somehow, I would keep my promise that Larry be buried at Arlington.

The next morning, I put on a black dress Mother had made for me when I was a senior in high school. I wore the Mikimoto pearl necklace Larry had bought on his R&R trip to Japan, along with some new pearl earrings Papa and Mama Hull gave me.

The funeral director pulled up out in front of Mother's home in the Singleton Funeral Home limo. He had buried my father, now he would direct the memorial service for my husband. He escorted Mrs. Locke, Mother, Larry's family, and me into the somber car. The rest of the family and close friends got into their cars, and we proceeded across town to the Seminole First Baptist Church.

I have very little memory of the service, except that I was acutely self-conscious. After all, I was a mental patient. I believed I had to be above all reproach. I had to remain in control, although inside I felt as if I would burst apart at the seams from sorrow.

I had been here before—at Daddy's funeral, fifteen years earlier. I remembered the afternoon before the funeral. While all the visitors and Mother were in the parlor at the funeral home, I sneaked into the room were Daddy lay, pulled a chair up to his casket, and kissed him good-bye. At the time, everyone, including

Mother, said he had gone to be with Jesus. I decided if things got too bad, I'd go be with Jesus and Daddy, too.

Now I stared at the flower arrangement I had designed for Larry. It seemed like a pitiful representation of who he was. He wasn't there at the front of the church, and we were in Seminole, Texas, not Arlington. *Larry, for now, this is the best I can do*, I whispered silently.

We had no body, but after the service we followed funeral protocol and went to the cemetery. As the limo pulled through the cemetery gates, I felt like I was home. As a teenager I had talked to Daddy numerous times at his gravesite, sitting on his bench. We turned the familiar corner onto the small road in front of Daddy's grave and stopped where the tent and plastic grass carpet were set up just two lots down from my father. Seven United States Air Force Honor Guard airmen charged with executing the three-volley salute stood waiting at ease in formation. The sounds of the guns firing and the beautiful, mournful "Taps" calmed my fears that we had not done enough to honor Larry.

After the salute, an officer stepped forward.

"On behalf of the president of the United States and a grateful nation, we offer this flag for the faithful and dedicated service of First Lt. James Larry Hull," the officer said somberly as he handed me the folded flag.

"On behalf of Larry's family," I whispered, "we thank you."

~~~~~~

NINETEEN

Bringing Home the Bacon

M rs. Locke and I flew back to Kansas after the memorial service. On the way home I was rude to her, although I didn't know why. Perhaps after being with Laura and coming to grips with the reality of my circumstances at home, I resented her constant supervision. Mrs. Locke's presence reminded me of how sick I had been, or maybe how sick I still was. Larry was gone. I had to grow up and be independent if I wanted to live with my daughter again.

Laura celebrated her second birthday on March fourth. I felt awful about not being there. I had given one baby up for adoption to make sure she would have a mother and a daddy. The irony that Laura would grow up without a father was excruciating. I recalled the days Mother and Daddy left me as a youngster. I felt awful leaving Laura, but she couldn't be with me while I was at Menninger.

~~~~~~

I spent Laura's birthday reliving the day I gave birth to her. She had arrived on a Tuesday. The weekend before, Larry had been watching Sunday night football while I put a roast in the oven and a load of clothes in the wash. I hadn't slept well the night before and decided a warm bath would do me good.

"Brrrrr!" Larry came in from the cold, stamping the snow from his boots. He'd gone to the laundry room in our duplex community to get the clothes from the dryer. "I'm glad we're tucked in and don't have to go out today," he teased, making sure I appreciated him for going to get the laundry.

I felt shaky and not myself, but I didn't think too much about it. When I started to get out of the bathtub, I slipped, catching myself on the edge of the tub. That seemed weird, but I didn't want to overreact. I put on a muumuu and slippers and cuddled up next to Larry on the sofa.

"Game's going good. My guys are gonna win. Just a little wager?" he asked.

"Larry, what's wrong with the television?" I ignored his hopeful request to bet on the game. "Is the weather making it blurry?"

Larry frowned. "What are you talking about? The picture's fine."

"Oh, nothing. It's probably just me. Got to go to the bathroom again. Comes with the territory." I smiled as I left the couch, but I didn't go to the bathroom. Instead, I slipped into our bedroom and called my OB.

"Dr. Shannon, something's wrong," I said when he answered. "I can't see so well. My vision's blurry, like when I had my first baby. And I'm a little dizzy." I whispered, not wanting to worry Larry.

"Tyra, listen carefully," the doctor urged. "Have Larry take you to the emergency room. I'll meet you there. Go now." He was emphatic.

Here we go again, I thought, remembering my first pregnancy. Both the baby and I had almost died from eclampsia. *God, I cannot lose this baby*, I pleaded as I put on jeans, a Tech sweatshirt, and my favorite pair of loafers and walked into the living room.

"I don't feel so good," I said to Larry as nonchalantly as I could manage. "I called Dr. Shannon. He wants us to meet him at the hospital. We better go. My bag's in the closet." It had been packed for days.

"Are you all right?" Larry looked worried. "I'll get my coat and pull the car up to the curb. Stay at the door until I come and get you. I'll walk you to the car. I mean it, stay inside."

We drove in silence to the hospital. Larry pulled up to the emergency room door, where Dr. Shannon was waiting for us. *Be steady, Tyra,* I told myself. *Don't worry Larry.* I remember getting into a wheelchair, then nothing more until I awoke, still pregnant, the next morning. I had toxemia, so Dr. Shannon had induced labor Sunday night. Mother had arrived from Seminole, but no baby.

Larry was nearing the end of pilot training, so he went back to work on Tuesday morning. Our baby girl was born later that day. Her daddy was in the clouds, figuratively and literally. Larry came to the hospital as soon as he got off work to meet his new daughter, grinning as if he was the luckiest man on earth. We decided to name her Laura Elizabeth Hull.

I was surprised when several of my relatives visited from out of town. Two days later, Mother explained they were in town for my twenty-year-old cousin's funeral. She had driven her car into a tree and died. I felt so sorry for my uncle. His two-year-old baby boy had drowned in a fishpond, and now his only other child was also gone. Larry and I were getting a new baby, yet Uncle Buddy's Cindy was dead. I tried to make sense of it. When Daddy died I'd heard one of the ladies from church say, "The Lord giveth and the Lord taketh away."

I didn't want to believe the Lord took Cindy so Larry and I could have our baby. *That woman didn't know what she was talking about,* I told myself. On the other hand, we had lost Daddy right before we got my baby sister, so maybe there was something to what the lady had said, after all.

~~~

My life had changed radically with the arrival of our daughter. Now that Larry had been killed, it was changing again. It was as if a switch inside me flipped to the "move forward" setting. My conversations with Dr. Roberts turned to making plans for Laura and me. I wanted to do better. Larry's voice inside my head assured me I could, and that he would never leave me.

On a walk with Dr. Roberts, I told him I didn't want to go back to Texas. "I want to move Larry's trailer—the one he bought in case he didn't come home—here, for Laura and me," I explained. "I want to finish my degree at Washburn and become a teacher like Larry and I planned."

Dr. Roberts listened, nodding from time to time.

"I'll need to make arrangements at Reese Air Force Base in Lubbock to have the trailer moved here." I had already thought this all through. "The air force will pay for it. The sergeant who took me to the base here to sign up for veterans' benefits told me. The air force will pay my tuition when I go back to school, and he showed me a new mobile home park near Forbes Air Force Base. They have a daycare center where Laura can stay. I've already visited with the childcare workers. She'll be in good hands while I'm at school. I'll go to the library to do my homework and study before I pick her up each day. That way, she'll have my undivided attention until she goes to bed at night. We'll have enough money to get by." I sounded like Larry explaining to Mother how we'd get by when we'd married.

"The air force will also pay for me to stay in the hospital until I'm discharged, and for my outpatient therapy afterwards," I added.

"It sounds like you've been doing your homework." Dr. Roberts seldom showed his emotions, yet he seemed pleased that I had started making plans. "I suggest you meet with the authorities in Lubbock to have your mobile home moved."

"Dr. Roberts, I know patients aren't supposed to have cars, but until the trailer gets here, I have things to do. I've got to see the registrar at Washburn and decide on a trailer park."

"We'll talk about that when the time comes," he assured me. "What about your classes here? Which ones do you think you can continue?"

"Between the calls I need to make and the trips with the sergeant, it's hard to go regularly. I'd like to keep gym if I can." I recalled my whiny attitude when I'd first learned I had to do anything physical at Menninger.

"Is that so, Mrs. Hull?" Dr. Roberts chuckled. "Why is that?"

"It's fun and my friends are there," I retorted, grinning.

As we walked back to the Clinic I said, "I do hope Laura and I can move to Topeka. I've missed her so much. Now that Larry's gone, I miss her even more."

"You're on the way to making that a reality, but take your time. No one is rushing you," he encouraged.

That was true, but I was on a mission. Larry was gone. The vows I had made to him were my blueprint; the coping strategies I had learned at Menninger my tools. It was time to build a life for Laura and myself without Larry.

~~~~~~~~

TWENTY

Discharged from Menninger

Shortly after my conversation with Dr. Roberts, I flew to Lubbock to finalize arrangements to move our trailer house to Topeka. I saw Laura briefly, then I bought a new car and followed our trailer to Kansas. I had a love/hate relationship with the trailer. It represented Larry's responsibility toward Laura and me, but it also reminded me that he had planned ahead for his death. I wondered if he'd had a premonition, or if it was just simply rational planning any young man would do before going to war.

Dr. Roberts recommended a transitional step to ease my move from inpatient hospitalization to outpatient therapy, so I continued to see my doctor and analyst at Menninger as well as eat meals and sleep there. Returning to Menninger at the end of each day felt like going home. Despite all the changes and stress, I wasn't tempted to binge or purge.

I made it a point to arrive back at the Clinic in time to join Penny, Deborah, and Forbes for dinner. Occasionally, Skylar sat with us, too. I would miss them all terribly once I left. They wanted to hear all about my plans—when I would move out of the Clinic for good and whether I had already enrolled at the university.

I was self-conscious and didn't want to act superior, so I downplayed my accomplishments, but not as much as I downplayed my fears. I only admitted to Mrs. Locke and Dr. Roberts that a big part of me was afraid of leaving the Clinic. I feared I couldn't handle it on the outside and might have to go back to Menninger. *That can't happen*, I'd tell myself when I started having those thoughts. *You are not going to let Laura down, no matter what.*

Larry's personal belongings finally arrived. As I unpacked them, I privately vowed that one day I'd contact Lieutenant Archer Battista, the Causality Assistance Officer (CAO) who'd shipped Larry's belongings home, to learn more about what had happened to Larry. The shipment included a TEAC reel-to-reel tape player accompanied by twenty-one double-sided tapes filled with music Larry had recorded from his brothers-in-arms' music collections, Panasonic headphones, and Pioneer speakers. I yearned for any connection with my husband.

I grew obsessed with Larry's music. With the headphones snug over my ears, I drowned out anything other than thoughts of him. I listened intently to every song, analyzing it as if it might contain a special message for me.

Late in the springtime, I moved completely into the trailer. I continued to see Dr. Roberts and my analyst, Dr. Fitzgerald, on an outpatient basis. I devised a strict schedule to control myself, so I wouldn't succumb to my old habits of staying in bed all day or binging and purging. The simplest things were the hardest, like making and eating meals and shopping for groceries. I had become accustomed to having my meals prepared for me. Making choices in grocery stores or from restaurant menus without the Menninger community around me was daunting. I feared going off the rails and piling Twinkies, half gallons of banana nut ice cream, jars of chili con queso, and multiple bags of Doritos in my shopping cart. Most of the time, I didn't give in.

Dr. Roberts had taught me that when I did have a slip, I should let it go and move on, rather than start a punishment loop where I gorged then purged, which made me sleep. When I slept, I was often unable to accomplish my work, and this caused me to gorge and then purge again.

Living alone was frightening, but I knew it meant I was better, or Dr. Roberts wouldn't have terminated my inpatient care. As soon as the school year ended and Mother could drive her up, Laura was coming to be with me. The prospect of having my daughter back kept me going more than anything else.

Around the same time, I was invited to a ceremony at Forbes Air Force Base to receive Larry's medals, awarded posthumously. The special ceremony was due to the high honor of Larry's medals, and I was encouraged to bring family or friends. I had no family in Topeka other than my fellow patients at Menninger. I asked Dr. Roberts if he could get passes for some of them to attend the ceremony with me, along with an aide to accompany those who couldn't leave unsupervised.

Members of the weller-than-well group, including Forbes and Deborah, Lainey, the aide, and I went to the ceremony in a Menninger van. I accepted the Silver Star (the third highest award for valor after the Air Force Cross and Medal of Honor), the Distinguished Flying Cross with one Oak Leaf Cluster, the Air Medal with eight Oak Leaf Clusters, and the Purple Heart, on Larry's behalf. I felt pride in Larry, mixed with gratitude for my Menninger family. Afterward, we went to the trailer for punch and cookies. They said they loved the house.

"I am so impressed Larry bought this for you and Laura," said Deborah, sincerely.

The Topeka Capital-Journal published a photograph of me accepting Larry's medals. This didn't soothe the part of me that was distraught about not keeping my promise to bury Larry at Arlington, but at least his valor and sacrifice had been acknowledged in print.

I flew to Texas to show Larry's medals to my family. On the way back to Menninger, passengers on the plane were discussing newspaper accounts of the first anniversary of the Kent State shootings.

Torn by the contradiction of those young people's deaths and the medals presented to me posthumously on behalf of my husband, I wondered why so many young Americans had to be killed before the Vietnam Conflict was resolved.

A couple weeks later, I had my last session with Dr. Roberts. We met in the cafeteria, got our traditional cup of coffee, and went for our walk.

"Where would you like to go?" he asked.

"To the rose garden." I smiled. "Do you remember how I couldn't stand the rose garden when I first came?"

"How could I forget, Mrs. Hull?" There was a twinkle in his eye.

"It reminded me of death, and I hated it."

"What's changed?" he coaxed.

"When I first came, the sweet smell of the roses made me ill. They symbolized death and reminded me of all the people in my family who had died. The roses haven't changed; what they symbolize for me has. They used to represent pain, but now they offer pleasure. I've learned through therapy how to look for new possibilities and new perspectives.

"The same thing's true of places, like Texas. And people, like some of my family. But I'm still working on those. Things are easier than people."

We sat quietly for a few moments. I remembered how Dr. Roberts's silence had agitated me when I first came to the Clinic. Now I found it comforting. "It may be outside the boundaries to say so, but I've felt loved here. Everyone has worked so hard to help me get better and I'm grateful.

"I've learned to enjoy beautiful things again. I can choose to change my perspective and the meaning of symbols in my life. Do you think that sounds corny, Dr. Roberts?" I searched his face, hoping he understood what I was trying to say.

"No, not corny, using your word. Sincere? Yes," he answered.

"Dr. Roberts, I think there's a scripture that says something like 'today we see darkly but one day we'll see clearly.' It's about how we see God as if through a smudged mirror, but one day we'll see Him clearly.

"Can I tell you what I really think?" I rushed ahead before he could answer. "I think seeing clearly means having hope. I think it's about changing your perspective to see the good, not just the bad. You can really get sick when you lose hope.

"Dr. Roberts, I think my clinical depression was a soul sickness. Do you?"

"Tell me more," he encouraged.

"I don't think you have it—I mean clinical depression—then you don't have it. You have to take care of yourself. It's a sliding scale. If you get too far down, you need help getting out of the dark."

He nodded. "Mrs. Hull, pay attention to your awareness. Pay attention to how you're feeling. If you need help, talk with Dr. Fitzgerald."

"I like Dr. Fitzgerald, but it's not the same as being with you. He doesn't talk through answers or help me make decisions. I'm afraid of not seeing you." Tears started to flow.

"Dr. Fitzgerald is an excellent analyst. We wouldn't recommend that you terminate your work with me if you weren't ready. It's natural to feel uncomfortable some days. If you feel like you need more help, you'll tell Dr. Fitzgerald, and he'll help you work through it.

"What will you do when you are aware you're seeing darkly, Mrs. Hull?" Dr. Roberts asked.

"I'll play with Laura. We'll go to the mall and be around people. I'll write it down, so I remember to tell Dr. Fitzgerald," I answered.

"And if you can't change your perspective, then what?" he probed harder.

"I won't eat and throw up, and I won't cut. I'll call someone, or take Laura to the park. Maybe by then, I'll know my neighbors and I'll knock on their door to borrow sugar, even though I don't need any. I'll do anything to be around people and not slide backwards.

"Do I sound like I'm ready to say good-bye?" I would miss dear Dr. Roberts terribly. If it hadn't been inappropriate, I would have thrown my arms around him and hugged him on behalf of Larry, Laura, and Daddy.

Looking at me with eyes that exuded honesty, Dr. Roberts said, "Yes, Mrs. Hull, you certainly do. It's hard for you, but that's normal. You've done well. I'll look forward to seeing you in the dining room or on the grounds. You should be proud of all you've accomplished."

TWENTY-ONE

Mother and Daughter Reunion

Laura was coming. On the day my mother and sister were bringing her to Kansas to live with me in the trailer house, I was beside myself with excitement and nervousness. I wondered if she would be happy with me after living with the Lamberts for almost nine months, nearly one-third of her entire life. I'd bought a huge teddy bear for her room and hung the plaque Nennie had bought over Laura's bed. *Tuesday's Child*, it said. Laura had been born on a Tuesday.

So much had happened since March 4, 1969. Though I hadn't wanted Larry to buy the trailer, I was grateful for it. Laura and I had a home he'd chosen for us. I put a photo of Larry on the dresser in Laura's room, the same one I had on my dresser. I'd also hung a photo of the three of us on her wall. I wanted to make sure she knew whom her daddy was and that he'd loved her.

The day dragged on as I waited for evening, when my mother and sister would drop Laura off. I revisited her room over and over, analyzing every detail, trying to make sure it was perfect for a two-year-old. The tiny blue and green bathing suit I'd purchased for the trips we would take to Lake Shawnee, a few miles from the trailer, was lying in her crib. I promised myself we would go on picnics at the lake and learn the names of the birds that lived in the huge green Kansas trees. Our new home was so unlike the barren sandy fields in West Texas.

I drove to the Clinic in time for lunch, hoping to meet up with some of my friends who were still patients. On the drive over, I wondered if Laura would like the food I'd bought for her. I'd spent the day before at the base, buying new outfits and grocery shopping, trying to do what I could to make her feel at home with me. I'd even bought two red roses, one for her and one for me. The small flower arrangement represented our little family.

The moment I entered the dining room, I relaxed. I was early and my friends weren't there yet, but I felt like I was home.

As I walked through the cafeteria line, one of the servers asked, "Your favorite spinach dish today?"

Grateful for the recognition, I chose my food and sat down across from a table of staff members. They waved hello. Mrs. Locke was with them, so I stepped over to the table and sat down in the empty chair next to her. "Guess who's coming today? Laura!" I beamed. For those who didn't know her I added, "My little girl."

"That's wonderful. You take care of yourself and that baby, but don't be a stranger," Mrs. Locke said. "I imagine she's grown since I met her at Larry's memorial service."

"I've only seen her once since then, after the medal ceremony," I said. "Mother says she's really getting tall."

Mrs. Locke turned to the rest of the table. "Laura is blond-haired and blue-eyed, like her daddy's photos."

To me she said again, "Don't be a stranger. Stay in touch. When do you start school?"

"Not 'til later in the summer. I want us to have a routine in place before I start." I'd made a point of discussing my plans and options with Mrs. Locke before making any major decisions.

What would I have done without Mrs. Locke and Dr. Roberts through all this? Thank God I had somewhere to go if I ever got in trouble.

I had an analysis appointment with Dr. Fitzgerald at 4:00 in a small building next to the Clinic. After lunch, while the others went to their classes or back to the unit, I killed time before my appointment by walking down to the pond. I remembered the day I'd thought I was losing it when I heard lions, tigers, and elephants. I'd thought it was all in my head. A ray of sunshine warmed me as I recalled my relief when Mrs. Locke told me there was a zoo across the street, hidden by the hedges and trees.

I rounded the corner of the pond and headed for the rose garden, where a few weeks before I had said good-bye to Dr. Roberts. I wished I could sit with him today instead of seeing Dr. Fitzgerald, but I knew that I needed to move on to the next step of my recovery.

Sitting in the garden, I thought about James Taylor's "Fire and Rain" and the night we learned Larry was dead. I hummed a few bars from "Joy to the World" by Three Dog Night, the song we listened to in the gym while playing volleyball. A few nights earlier, it had played on one of the tapes Larry had recorded.

Music soothed me. It must have done the same for Larry. I'd play his music for Laura. We'd dance to her daddy's music together. *She'll be here soon*, I thought. I couldn't wait.

When I entered Dr. Fitzgerald's office I said, "Laura will be here when we finish today."

"Yes, I know." He nodded. "How do you feel about that?"

"Nervous, excited, and a little scared," I replied, "I'm ready. Her room's ready. She'll be here in just one more hour."

"It's a special day. Something would be wrong if you weren't a bit apprehensive. Your mother's bringing her here after our appointment, is that right?"

"Yes. I don't think I can concentrate on our conversation," I said. "But arrangements for me to start classes at Washburn later in the summer are finalized, and Laura's all set up to go to day care at the base when I start school this summer. I'm going to take her to the care center several times before school starts, so she'll feel comfortable once she has to stay the whole day. I hope Larry would approve. I never imagined I'd be moving Laura and me to Kansas when I first came to Menninger. I'm really so grateful Larry bought that trailer. I wish I had been more grateful when he bought it instead of complaining that I didn't want to live in a trailer.

"Dr. Fitzgerald, what if Laura's homesick for the Lamberts or Mother?" What if she would rather be with them? I finally admitted my fear at the end of the appointment.

"I've been away for almost nine months and haven't seen her except for when I went home for Larry's memorial service and after the medal ceremony. We barely spent time together then, so much was going on."

"Just be you," he encouraged as we wrapped up our session. "I'm confident Laura will be pleased to be with you. Enjoy this special time. You can tell me all about it at your next appointment."

I stepped out of the door and looked over at the circle drive. Standing in front of the car was Mother, my sister, and Laura, who was jumping up and down. Mother was holding her hand. Laura was precious in a cute little sundress, her hair in ponytails. As I walked toward the car, Laura let go of Mother's hand and ran to me.

"Mommy, Mommy!" she cried as I knelt down. She jumped into my arms, and we hugged each other tight. Laura was home. My heart burst as I whispered to Larry, *I'll never leave her again. I promise.*

Mother left on Sunday, but my sister stayed for a week. Then finally, Laura and I were alone. She seemed to recognize the trailer, though I couldn't imagine how. It had been almost a year since we'd lived there with Larry, and we'd only been in it a few days.

I didn't start classes until the second summer session, so we had time to establish a routine. I took Laura to the daycare center on the base when I had appointments with Dr. Fitzgerald. I usually went for lunch at Menninger first, so I could spend time with my friends there and so Laura could get acclimated to the daycare center before I started classes at the university. I shopped at the Base Exchange and Commissary. In addition to Menninger and the trailer house, the base was another place that felt familiar.

I felt at home there. Larry and I had lived in base housing while he was in pilot training at Reese, and being on the base made me feel close to him.

Weekends were a challenge, just as they had been while I was hospitalized. But I had learned to make plans and to keep busy. Saturday mornings, after I dressed Laura, we'd go to the base to shop for groceries and other items. I took great care to dress her in cute outfits with color-coordinated bows for her ponytails. She was precious and always drew attention from other shoppers. Sooner or later, someone would ask about her daddy—what did he do on base, what was his assignment? Eventually, I was able to tell people about losing Larry in Vietnam without crying. Some offered condolences and others looked at Laura and me with pity. I hated pity, though I told myself they meant well.

After grocery shopping, we'd go home, and I'd study while Laura took a nap. Our Saturday night ritual involved dinner at the Steak and Ale restaurant on Topeka Boulevard not far from our trailer park. It was a nice restaurant and reminded me of a favorite steak house Larry and I used to go to for dinner. Laura and I shared a filet mignon, baked potato, and salad. It was our night out almost every weekend. Afterward, I'd put her to bed, then I'd put Larry's music on, put the headphones over my ears, and fall asleep on the living room floor.

We started attending an American Baptist church close to Menninger on Sunday mornings. I liked this church, because it reminded me of home and because there was less talk about the devil and hell there than at the church I'd attended as a child. I knew Mother and my sister were probably in church at the same time. Somehow, that made me feel less lonely. After church, we'd go to the Red Dragon Chinese restaurant. We saved our rolls for the ducks at the pond in the cemetery across the street from Menninger.

Some weekday evenings, we went to a local restaurant known for its hot dogs. They had a jukebox, and Laura loved to put a coin in and play "Take Me Home, Country Roads." She'd sing at the top of her lungs and dance to the music if it wasn't crowded. I worried about her disturbing the other customers, but that didn't seem to be a problem since they egged her on.

After a few months, a young couple with a little boy about Laura's age parked their trailer house next to ours. Laura enjoyed Billy, and his mother often invited her to play with him when I had to study. By the time my classes began at Washburn, Laura and I had established enough rituals to get us through the weekends.

We traveled to Seminole the Christmas after I moved out of Menninger. It was good to be with my family. They had missed Laura especially and were thrilled to have us there for the holidays, but I was relieved when we left. Topeka was home now. Laura and I were happy there, although I was lonely and missed Larry.

My relationship with my husband changed with his death, but I felt his spirit close by. I was still distressed that I hadn't kept my promise that he would be buried at Arlington, but in my heart I believed that somehow I would keep it one day. I had said goodbye to Texas but not to Larry. His music brought him close to me every night, encouraging me to do my best. Wherever I went, he would always be there, too.

~~~~~~~~~~

TWENTY-TWO

You Have to Go Back

Not long after the new year, in early 1972, a woman in one of my night classes invited me and one of her husband's unmarried friends over for dinner. I was reluctant to accept the invitation, but decided an evening with grown-ups would be good for me. The husband's friend, Kenneth, was seven years older than me. Warm and engaging, he had grown up in the Midwest and worked in the fashion industry. It felt strange to be at dinner with a couple and a man who wasn't Larry, but it was good to spend an evening out.

We went on a tour of my friend's new home and took a quick peek at their little boy, asleep in the nursery upstairs. I was impressed with Kenneth's genuine interest in the new parents' up-to-the-minute account of their baby's development.

The following weekend, I invited Kenneth over to the trailer. Soon, he became a part of our lives and even watched Laura while I attended night classes. When I returned to pick her up after class, he'd holler, "Be careful when you open the door! Don't step on the giraffes or the other animals in our zoo." I'd find the two of them sitting among a maze of huge pillows arranged like cages for their imaginary animals.

Sometimes I felt disloyal to Larry, but I was impressed with Laura and Kenneth's relationship. He was good to my daughter, as well as to me. I wondered how Larry would feel if I were serious about another man. I still felt him nearby, still heard his encouraging voice in my mind. I cared for Kenneth deeply and tried to push Larry out of my thoughts, but he was never far away.

I was so thrilled for my daughter to have such a wonderful father figure in her life that when Kenneth asked me to marry him, I said yes. Our wedding day was bittersweet. I couldn't help thinking about the wedding vows I'd made to Larry. "'Til death do us part" gave me permission to move on with my life, but Larry had only been dead for a year and a half. Selling the trailer he had bought for us felt like a betrayal, but I did it anyway, and Laura and Kenneth and I moved into a new house.

Once the three of us settled in, I focused on my career. I had finished my bachelor's degree in education and was hired to teach social studies at East Topeka Junior High in a predominately black neighborhood. Ninety-seven percent of our students were minorities. I loved the job, the students, and the community. Those children taught me to teach. They teased me sometimes about my pronounced Texas twang, but over time, they embraced me.

Another first-year teacher from Little Rock, Arkansas, and I became good friends. She was African-American and had seen the chaos that erupted when Central High School was integrated and the National Guard was called in. We developed a team-teaching class called "Self-Expression through Communication and Social Interaction." It integrated current events and literature about individuals who had made a difference in our country with the required social studies and English curriculum. Social activism and individualism were rampant in the midseventies—the Kent State student protests, the Civil Rights Movement, labor union demands, feminism, and environmentalism all came to the fore-front of the national scene. Rather than parades of people waving flags and celebrating our heroes, protests against the Vietnam War and disrespect toward returning soldiers was the norm until the war finally ended in 1975. We wanted to teach children to think and to consider the effects of leaders who had made a difference. Our lessons on the importance of looking beyond labels to the character of each individual impressed our students so much that they reversed their nicknames for us, calling me "Pepper" and my African-American colleague "Salt."

I loved teaching, but I wanted to be a principal. In 1974, I enrolled in a master's degree program in school administration at the University of Kansas in Lawrence, about twenty miles from Topeka. I took classes at night. In the fall of 1976, I was appointed Middle School Coordinator for the school district and continued teaching part-time at East Topeka Junior High. By 1977 I had completed my master's and immediately enrolled in the doctoral program.

One afternoon in January 1978, as I was on my way to pick up Claudia with whom I carpooled to KU, I marveled over the fact that I was working on my doctorate. I recalled the difficulty I'd faced as an adolescent and my habit of skipping classes in high school. Several teachers back then had taken an interest in me and given me the benefit of the doubt when I hadn't earned it. Their attitude made a monumental difference in my ability to hang on and not give up completely during those turbulent teen years. They may have even saved me. I promised God that afternoon, *If I can be a principal, I will give back.* I desperately wanted to make a difference, especially for children who didn't win accolades, blue ribbons, or honors. I hoped that perhaps I could even make up for some of the trouble I'd caused.

We were already at KU that winter night when university officials canceled all remaining classes due to hazardous weather conditions. Claudia and I left for Topeka on 45, the two-lane state highway. I drove while Claudia rode in the passenger seat. Three miles west of Lawrence, we were hit head-on when a drunk driver crossed the center line into our lane. The driver of the oncoming car, a young man in his early twenties, was killed. His passenger sustained a broken leg. Claudia broke her right elbow and some of her front teeth.

I wasn't as fortunate as my friend. I watched from somewhere above myself as a parade of emergency vehicles arrived, red lights flashing. As rescuers worked the scene below, I focused on my body, which was trapped in the bucket seat, lodged between the doorframe and the windshield.

Larry's voice, initially faint and distant, grew stronger as he called my name repeatedly. Though transfixed by the accident, I was distracted by his voice, which emanated from the intense, brilliant light and comforting warmth that surrounded me. Larry was with me. I could feel him.

"Tyra, you have to go back. You have to go back and take care of Laura." He spoke firmly, yet soothingly. "You have to go back and take care of Laura."

I wanted to go with Larry more than anything, but he was right. Laura needed me more.

Emergency teams removed me from the car with the Jaws of Life. I was aware that they were having a difficult time of it, and I sensed that if they weren't able to get me out, I'd have no choice but to go with Larry. I wanted them to be successful. I wanted to take care of Laura, not leave her alone without either of us. After several attempts, I was finally pulled, unconscious, from the wreckage.

Twelve days later, as I awoke in the ICU, I slipped away from a host of butterflies with wings of brilliant gold and rainbow hues, escorting me back to consciousness. As I opened my eyes, I looked around the tiny room, hoping Larry was still with me. He was gone. I savored his visit and kept it to myself. I was elated that he still loved Laura and me enough to show up when I'd been in mortal danger. I was grateful to be alive and believed Larry had given the doctors an opportunity to save my life.

I was also furious with him. How dare he tell me to go back and live when he had left us to volunteer for one of the most dangerous assignments in the United States Air Force during the Vietnam War? It was the first time I could remember feeling completely and utterly irate toward him—not just angry, but enraged.

Feeling anger toward Larry was uncomfortable. I couldn't remember ever being really angry with him while we were together. I recalled the day he left for Vietnam, how frightened I was for him to leave, and how scared I was that he wouldn't come home. I'd wanted to beg him to stay. But I didn't, since I knew how much his dream of flying in the air force meant to him. I didn't give him the chance to change his mind. I hadn't told him how ill I really was, and I downplayed my fear when he asked how I was feeling. A part of me held it against him that he had left for Vietnam and followed his dream. I realized that I had to accept what had happened and forgive him. It would take time—years, in fact. It was so hard to admit my anger toward Larry for getting killed and leaving us, but acknowledging it was a beginning. Each time those feelings surfaced, I promised Larry that I would get better, take care of Laura, and complete my doctoral studies.

~~~~~

It was against hospital policy for children to be allowed in patient rooms, but one day, Kenneth brought Laura to visit me in the hospital waiting room. We were thrilled to see each other. Once she saw I was going to be okay, she was upset that so many visitors had autographed my casts before she'd had the chance. I'd promised Larry I would go home and take care of Laura. *One more time, you've left her*, I chastised myself. *What if you'd been killed?* I started to wonder whether I was getting clinically depressed again, if my conversations with Larry were too frequent, and whether I depended on him too much. I promised myself that as soon as I was able, I'd make an appointment with my former social worker at Menninger. I needed to tell someone who wouldn't think I was completely out of my mind about being with Larry at the accident, how he'd insisted I go back and take care of Laura. But I'd have to wait. I had suffered a broken left foot, a crushed ankle on the right leg, and a fractured left wrist. In order to go home, I had to learn to walk using crutches.

Bill, my physical therapist, had nailed a piece of wood horizontally to the top of my left crutch, making a platform for my casted arm. He attached a wooden stick at the end of the platform for me to grip with my fingers. Two Velcro straps were attached to the underside of the platform, one for the elbow and the other for the wrist. I'd control my left crutch with my forearm. With a plastic boot slipped over the cast on my left leg, I could bear weight on that side.

I had a plaster cast on my right leg up to my knee. I used the other crutch to hold my weight on that side, as I could not use my right leg. Bill held on to a safety belt, strapped around my waist to keep me from falling. I was supposed to pull myself out of the wheelchair to standing and then walk with the help of the crutches. My left side was hard to control. The crutch with my forearm strapped to the platform on top often swung out from under me. Without Bill and my safety belt, I would have fallen to the linoleum floor in a heap of crutches, plaster casts, and a flailing arm. I felt helpless, clumsy, and out of control. Determined and stubborn, I was hard on myself. *I can't go home until I walk with these contraptions. I'll try harder next time,* I'd swear privately. Sometimes I'd just swear.

I went to physical therapy twice a day, napping between the morning and afternoon sessions. Bill taught me how to get into the wheelchair, strap on my left crutch, get out of the chair, and walk. The goal was for me to get from the bed to the wheelchair to the bathroom, then back to bed again. Once I reached that level of independence, I could go home.

Like a small child, I learned to balance, fall, get back up, and do it over and over again. Mother's notorious admonishment from childhood surfaced in my mind: *The least you can do is look right and act right.* I focused my energy on doing what I needed to do. I contacted my professors, both of whom gave me permission to continue taking classes while I recuperated. In one class, my classmates submitted their notes to the professor, who forwarded them to me along with a recording of each lecture. I promised myself I would catch up with my classmates and walk—even if it had to be on crutches—into class at KU to take both finals at the end of the semester.

TWENTY-THREE

One More Burden

I returned home in a wheelchair, still wearing casts on three of my four limbs. Eight-year-old Laura wanted to sit in my lap, but that was physically impossible. She finally settled for scrunching up close to my right side, so I could put my arm around her for a long hug.

Berne, a home healthcare aide, came daily to help me while Kenneth worked and Laura went to school. I spent most mornings working on school assignments. Around 10:00 I began counting down to noon. Lunch included one sandwich and two beers.

Drinking made me feel like I had a shred of independence left. It was an act of defiance in response to my inability to go to the bathroom by myself or walk across the floor without Berne holding on to the safety belt to keep me from falling.

I wrestled with guilt, tormented with the knowledge that the twenty-one-year-old driver who had crashed head-on into my car was dead. If only I'd taken the interstate, I wouldn't have been in his way. He might still be alive. I thanked God I hadn't been the one drinking that day. But now, drinking a couple of beers at lunch was the only thing that diminished the incessant, torturous chatter in my head. One question rolled through my head, breaking over and over like waves: *Why am I always the one left?*

I spent several months recuperating, then I returned to work in a wheelchair. In the fall of 1978, I was hired as principal for Boswell Junior High. I was surprised when my former analyst, social worker, and a hospital aide from Menninger all walked in to enroll their children on the first day of school. Initially I was intimidated, but I could not have had a more supportive group of parents in my corner. The school's PTO president was also connected to the Clinic; she was married to one of the administrators. We became close friends, but I didn't tell her I had been a patient at Menninger seven years earlier.

My role as principal was perfect for me. I looked forward to going to work every day. The school was rich with children from diverse backgrounds, and the teachers were first class and committed. Most of all, I was fortunate to have an experienced assistant principal who mentored me and taught me how to be an administrator.

Life was full with work, completing the requirements for my doctorate, and getting treatment for my right ankle, which wasn't healing and was still in a cast. Kenneth took on most of the parenting duties for Laura, and I was grateful for his help. I had so many of the things I had hoped for, yet I wasn't happy. Hearing Larry's voice at the accident made me want to travel in time, back to when we were married. Many nights after driving back from my graduate classes at KU, I went down to our basement with several beers and listened to his tapes. I would drink until I fell asleep. Some nights it took two or three beers, others more like four or five. Drinking for me was a kind of group activity, attended by my child self; my rebellious, sneering teenager; and the determined, driven young widow full of judgment and resentment that I had grown into.

I asked Kenneth for a divorce the summer of 1979. Our relationship suffered from my ongoing medical issues, work and school schedules, and drinking, but most of all from my inability to let go of Larry. His presence at the accident brought the unfinished business regarding his death back to the center of my life. Laura was ten years old and heartbroken, but Kenneth stayed close to her, which made me feel less guilty about leaving the marriage.

~~~

When Laura was in seventh grade, one of her teachers, a self-described anti-war advocate, challenged Laura's portrayal of her father as an American hero in a speech she presented to her class. Several of Laura's classmates echoed their parents' opinions that Vietnam veterans were "baby killers." This was the impetus for me to find out if more information about Larry's death was no longer classified and now available.

The official regret letter delivered to me at Menninger in 1971 had said only that Larry's plane had gone down in South Vietnam. It had no details about the circumstances surrounding his final mission, other than that his death was apparently instantaneous, and extensive hostile fire prevented the ability to provide any more information. Another official letter followed two days later. A second attempt to recover Larry's remains from the wreckage was called off due to extreme hostile fire, and it appeared impossible to make any further recovery attempts in the near future. I'd received a third letter a few days later, informing me that Larry's aircraft had been totally destroyed by fire on February 22. His body was not coming home.

I searched through all the documents I had received from the air force over the last ten years, until I found the single page torn from a legal pad that had Archer Battista's contact information scribbled on it. He was the Casualty Assistance Officer who had shipped Larry's personal effects home. I tracked Archer down at a law firm on the East Coast. He flew in the air force reserves and offered to arrange a trip to Topeka over a weekend. When I told

Laura he was coming, she was miffed that she would not be going to dinner with Archer and me. I promised that I'd try to arrange breakfast for the three of us so she could meet him, too, but I had heard about veterans afflicted with post-traumatic stress, and I wanted to meet him alone first.

I regretted not bringing Laura along almost immediately after Archer and I sat down for dinner. Attentive and kind, Archer had been a comrade of Larry's from the time Larry arrived in Nam until Larry was killed. I wanted to know everything Archer could remember about Larry and their time together in the war. He told me that in the beginning he and Larry had flown the same kind of missions, but Larry later volunteered for a secret assignment. Archer didn't know any of the details.

I was stunned. What had Larry been doing on those secret missions? Archer encouraged me to contact the air force again, since information had become declassified.

Laura was waiting for me when I returned home that night. She was excited to hear she and I had a date with Archer the next morning at the Holiday Inn before he flew home. The next morning, we didn't talk much on the way to breakfast. As we got out of the car, I felt a shiver go up my spine. I had talked to Laura about her daddy all the time since she was a toddler, but I felt anxious about how she'd react to meeting someone who had flown with her father and had known him well.

When we walked in the door of the restaurant, my typically reserved teenager ran toward Archer, who was waiting for us in his air force flight suit. She threw her arms around his waist and hugged him tight. Archer hugged her back, as I stood there, stunned. She hadn't seen Larry since she was sixteen months old. She couldn't possibly remember him in a flight suit. Yet it was as if Archer's uniform was a magnet drawing her to him. She had run into his arms the same way she used to do when Larry came home from the flight line.

After we met Archer, a new urgency to know what had happened to Larry began to occupy my thoughts. Not long after this meeting, I spoke with an official in the Casualty Division at Randolph Air Force Base in San Antonio who told me that, based upon research and review of aircraft operational reports after the ending of hostilities, it was determined that Larry's plane went down in Laos, not in South Vietnam as originally reported. The error occurred because Larry's plane had crashed so close to the border between the two countries.

Around this same time, I admitted to myself that I had a problem with alcohol. I was still drinking beer daily, mostly at night after I came home from work. In an effort to control my drinking, I switched from beer to wine. Gin and tonics came next. It didn't matter what kind of alcohol I drank, the result was the same: I couldn't stop. Nothing I did kept my drinking in check. A run-in with the police resulted in a reckless driving charge, and I had to attend driving school. A woman from an anonymous support group spoke about her drinking and told us how she'd quit and what her life was like now that she was sober. She was clean, well dressed, and articulate—not my stereotypical notion of a drunk. She used the word *addiction*. As I listened to her, I knew in my heart I was addicted, too. After I heard her story, drinking was never the same. The buzz was there, but alcohol was no longer an antidote for fear and anxiety. Drinking had become one more burden.

I'd been appointed director of personnel for the school district in 1982. The position included helping faculty members who were coping with personal difficulties gain access to the Employees' Assistance Program. Ironically, I was extremely successful at convincing others to take advantage of the anonymous counseling program, which provided support for personal issues, including drinking problems.

It was impossible for me to deny my own problem any longer. I was functioning well during the day but drinking myself into oblivion every night after Laura went to bed. I called a friend who was involved with an anonymous support group for alcoholics trying to get sober, and told her about my drinking habits and my inability to quit on my own. When she asked if I would like to speak with a recovering alcoholic from the group, I didn't hesitate. I had promised Larry I would take care of Laura, but I was barely taking care of myself.

I met with two women in the group. Both of them were non-judgmental, and I appreciated that. They shared stories of how bad their drinking had been and how they got sober, then they invited me to a group meeting. Like the woman at the driving school, there was something in both of their stories that resonated with me. I was like them; I couldn't stop drinking on my own.

Although I was fearful about maintaining my anonymity, I agreed to attend a meeting for alcoholics and their families. I sat down with Laura and said, "I have to tell you something. I have a drinking problem. I've tried to quit, but I can't stop by myself."

"I know, Mom. I live with you," she quipped, looking at me as if I were stating the obvious. "Did you think it was a secret?" She wasn't rude, just incredulous that I thought I'd kept it from her. She agreed to go with me to an open meeting for people who were trying to quit drinking.

At my first meeting, I was consumed by overwhelming fear and shame, stunned by the number of people I knew, and stricken with fear of what they thought about me being there. The stories the three recovering alcoholics shared had mostly convinced me that the meeting, held in a church, would not include the threats I recalled from the sermons of my childhood, which promised hellfire and damnation for those who drank. Still, it was all I could do to stay in my chair. I wanted to run, but instead I gulped down cup after cup of coffee. When we held hands at the end and said the Serenity Prayer, I felt a sudden rush of peace. Nennie had taught me this prayer when I was fifteen. Thank God for my grandmother. She had been my best supporter throughout my childhood and my brief years with Larry.

Before going to bed that night, I read from the group's literature and said the Serenity Prayer five times aloud, as my new mentor had instructed. She also told me to go to meetings with other new members. "Hearing some of their stories will make you grateful," she advised.

I thought of Nennie when I prayed for serenity, courage, and wisdom. I wondered who had taught her the Serenity Prayer. Even when PaPa was killed in a tractor accident she had relied on the prayer. She had lived through her own challenging times and relied on the prayer. I would do well to do the same.

A few weeks later, I went to a meeting held in the office of a used car lot, where I immediately felt at home. Daddy had sold cars for a living, and so had I over the summers when I needed money for graduate school. A wave of fear washed over me as I entered the small, crowded room. I recognized one of the men as the parent of a former student. Although he nodded hello as I came in, I could tell that he hadn't recognized me. He was just being courteous, and I felt relieved.

The leader was a gruff old guy with yellowish-white hair. He greeted us and pointed to coffee supplies on the desk, the only permanent piece of furniture in the room. The coffee setup was the same as the one in the Menninger patient lounge. As I lowered myself into one of the metal folding chairs and lit a cigarette, I thought of my days there with gratitude.

"Welcome to tonight's meeting," the leader began. "Everything that's said here stays here." Introductions came next, and soon it was my turn. My voice trembled when I said my name. I planted my feet flat on the floor to steady myself. I'd been to several meetings by then, but I was still fearful of losing my anonymity and uncomfortable with calling myself an alcoholic. As the others spoke, I wondered how I could have ended up there. It wasn't the kind of place I had imagined I would be sitting once I earned my doctorate degree, or after I'd "graduated" from Menninger. But as I listened to their stories, I knew I was where I belonged.

One man spoke about having no job, losing his family, and not knowing where his next meal was coming from. I felt guilty for being ungrateful. I had heard people say they had been on the pity pot and felt sorry for themselves. For the first time, I realized that description fit me. I could sit on the pity pot the rest of my life and never accomplish my promises to Larry and myself. I had empathy for the homeless man, and for a few minutes, I quit thinking about my own problems.

I yearned to believe God was with me, even after all I had done wrong. Perhaps I could reconnect with such a God if I could get past my sadness and anger. I had once told Dr. Roberts that I thought my clinical depression was a soul sickness. Alcoholism was, too. I hadn't taken a drink since my first meeting, but I wasn't sure I could keep it up. After four weeks of sobriety, I felt hopeless, exhausted, and afraid that I couldn't stop for good. *Each day, don't drink, read the books, say Nennie's Serenity Prayer five times out loud, and go to meetings to be with people,* I'd tell myself repeatedly. I whined to my mentor—not because I wanted to drink, but because I hated the fear and anxiety I felt when I didn't.

The group said I could lean on them. That much I could do. That night, I started to feel more at home at the meetings. Tears ran down my face as we said the prayer. I felt a spiritual presence

Nennie's iris, 1954

Cessna O-2A flown by 1st Lt. Hull in Laos, 1970–1971

Larry's new sideburns, Da Nang, 1971

Laura and Tyra, 1972

MIA 1st Lt. James L. Hull comes home,
Arlington National Cemetery, November 2006

Rolling Thunder, Arlington National Cemetery, 2006

Seven Honor Guard airmen execute the three-volley salute for Lt. Larry Hull, Arlington National Cemetery, 2006

Presentation of the flag to Laura Hull,
Arlington National Cemetery, 2006

Retired Colonel Yarborough says good-bye to his friend and brother-in-arms,
1st Lt. James L. Hull, Arlington National Cemetery, 2006

Tyra's final good-bye, Arlington National Cemetery, 2006

Tyra's doctoral regalia,
Dominican University, River Forest, IL, 2007

Larry in his dress blues

among us. Some said they had found peace with God. Maybe I would, too.

When I started to leave, the old yellow-haired guy said, "Hope we'll see your dragging ass around here again."

"I'll be back," I said and managed a grin.

After the meeting, I went for coffee with some of the ladies. They usually ordered something to eat. Since I'd stopped drinking, my old addiction of binging and purging had returned, not often, but enough so that it scared me. After most meetings, I would have a piece of pie or bowl of ice cream before I went home. I tried not to stick my finger down my throat afterward. I considered drinking a step up from bulimia. At the very least, it seemed more socially acceptable. When I started making myself throw up again, I wondered if I was regressing. *At least you can't get arrested for gorging and purging*, I told myself, feeling grateful that I didn't feel the urge to cut.

~~~~~~~~~~

TWENTY-FOUR

Volunteering at the VA

After a year of sobriety, I was invited to volunteer on the alcohol treatment unit at the local VA hospital. Although I was nervous, I was also eager to share my story with veterans struggling to get sober, and, short on humility, I jumped at the opportunity to help them.

I felt an immediate kinship with the Vietnam veterans, who were the majority of those on the ward. Visiting and occasionally playing checkers was my entrée into one-on-one conversations with the patients. My introduction went something like this: "I'm Tyra, I've been sober a year, and I'm a Vietnam widow." It was an icebreaker. Most of our conversations moved from who they were, their branches of service, and where they'd been stationed, on to stories about their estranged families and friends.

They were also very curious about Larry.

"He was First Lt. James L. Hull, an air force pilot stationed in Da Nang," I usually began. "He was shot down in Laos. When his plane crashed, there was a fire at the site. His body was irretrievable due to heavy enemy fire. Before he left for duty, I promised him he would be buried at Arlington if he didn't come home, but I don't even know for certain where his plane went down. I'd do anything to keep that promise," I lamented.

I felt a strong bond with most of the vets I met. I had not experienced the horror of battle, put my life on the line, or been spit on by Americans who didn't agree with the war after returning home from serving our country. But the war had taken loved ones from all of us. Many of us were unable to grieve or cope, so we escaped our pain by drinking ourselves into oblivion. Alcohol had gotten some of us into trouble with the law, and most of our relationships with family and friends were difficult or nonexistent.

Things came to a head one night at a meeting at the VA hospital, which was open to alcoholics from the larger Topeka community as well as to patients. It was a speaker meeting, and the leader invited me to tell my story—what had happened and what my life was like now. Getting to know the men and hearing their stories had unlocked the stronghold on my emotions, especially my anger and fear. That night, I told them how grief over Larry had brought the overwhelming pain of losing Daddy to the surface. The two losses were linked together forever in a kind of "pain chain."

As I spoke that night, haunting secrets spilled out, along with a tally of the wrongs I had committed over the years. Except for my short time with Larry, I had abused alcohol since age fourteen. Everyone in the room listened as I sobbed. I spoke about my shame over being ungrateful for the trailer house Larry had bought for Laura and me before he went to Vietnam. Larry had bought it so Laura and I would own a place to live if he were killed, but all my life I'd heard that only poor white trash lived in trailer houses.

I finally pulled myself together enough to express my gratitude for the group, my sobriety, and the invitation to share. After I finished speaking, almost everyone in the room came to the podium and hugged me. They told me to keep coming to the meetings. Though comforted by the support, I was shaken to the core. I hadn't expected to fall apart in public. My tears and lack of control over my emotions shocked me. I was enormously angry, though not with anyone in particular. It was the first real step toward really feeling my grief over Larry and living with it. At Menninger, I'd been able to grieve my father, but when Larry was killed, I'd had to pull myself together to take care of Laura and go back to school. I really hadn't given myself the space to grieve Larry. Since his body wasn't returned to us, it made it easier to deny the loss, especially when I drank.

After the meeting at the Veteran's Administration, I contacted the Menninger Clinic's alcoholism unit and began outpatient therapy with Nolan Brohaugh, the social worker on my intake team when I was hospitalized at Menninger. He helped me confront my use of alcohol to avoid the pain of unfinished past losses. I had volunteered to help the veterans recover from their addiction. In turn, they were one of the most significant catalysts in my own recovery.

TWENTY-FIVE

Welcome Home Parade, Chicago

In 1984, Laura and I moved to Illinois, where I became director of instruction in a Chicago suburb, Highland Park. Both of us loved books, and we'd often make a trek to the Borders at the mall on weekends for shopping and an early dinner. After browsing among the stacks of new releases, we'd swing through the Vietnam section to see if there was anything on the shelves reporting new information that hadn't been previously available. I still knew almost nothing about Larry's case, except that his plane had crashed in Laos. But facts about the war that were once classified were being declassified.

One Saturday in 1986, fifteen years after Larry's death, Laura noticed a book with a bright orange cover titled *The Vietnam War*. I flipped through it. The author had included a list of soldiers still unaccounted for. It listed Larry in the MIA section rather than with the KIAs.

Maybe he's not dead, I thought. *Oh my God, what if he's alive?*

My mind reeled with questions. How could Larry be MIA, not KIA? Tempted to succumb to the fantasy that he might still be alive, I wrote to the publisher, seeking an explanation and accusing them of sensationalizing aspects of the war and causing my daughter and me more heartache. I added that I was sure we were not the only family who would be distressed if they were in our same circumstances and read the book.

The managing editor wrote me an apologetic letter, explaining that since a complete list of the unaccounted in the Vietnam Conflict had not appeared in any commercial publication, the company was committed to publishing their names.

I immediately called air force officials, who informed me that the misunderstanding occurred because Larry's remains had not been recovered. But there was no question: Larry had been killed. He was officially KIA.

~~~

Later in 1986, fifteen years after Larry's death, a friend invited me to the Chicago Vietnam Veterans Welcome Home Parade. The parade was three miles long. News broadcasts reported 200,000 marchers and almost 500,000 spectators. I squeezed through tightly packed bodies to get curbside on Michigan Avenue at Grant Park. It was a gorgeous, clear day. I looked around, breathing air thick with emotion, astounded by the massive crowd celebrating the sacrifice of our veterans.

Over a decade after the war had officially ended, Chicago finally acknowledged Vietnam veterans and their families. Larry and his fellow soldiers, including my brother, Rodney, who'd served a year in the navy commandeering two Patrol Torpedo boats on the Mekong River Delta and was awarded a Purple Heart, were being honored. Rodney and Larry had been close during the short time after Rodney came back from Vietnam and before Larry deployed to Da Nang. The demonstration of love and goodwill toward the veterans felt like a baptism, washing away the spittle and filthy names hurled at so many of them when they had returned home. Some former war protesters participated too, crying and hugging veterans, who hugged them back. A man in uniform saw me crying on the street corner. He came over and put his hands on my shoulders and said, "Welcome home. Did you lose someone?"

I collapsed into his arms, and he held me until I had to let go to breathe. It was a momentous day, one in which I shed another layer of hurt. But it was a different kind of healing, the kind that comes when you're acknowledged, when what you've lost is no longer invisible.

I imagined Larry walking in the parade. I imagined it so hard I began to believe it was possible and started looking for him. I forced myself back into reality. I stood in line to find Larry's name on The Moving Wall, a replica of the original in Washington. I had never seen his name on any permanent public monument or head-stone. Tracing my fingers over the letters in his name verified that First Lt. James L. Hull was dead. Larry was a hero. His name was on the Vietnam Veterans Memorial in Washington, DC. I promised myself I'd take Laura there as soon as possible.

~~~

In the spring of 1987, half asleep in that twilight space between dreaming and the reality of a new day, I fumbled for my ringing phone. It was only 5:00 in the morning. Phone calls in the early morning hours usually heralded bad news.

It was Mother. "Tyra, Rodney's dead. Your brother's dead," she sobbed.

"Mother, what happened?" I tried to stay calm, but the sound of Mother's tears made me want to cry, too.

"He was having a balloon procedure and had a heart attack right there on the table. Oh, Tyra, can you come?" she pleaded. This was not the stoic mother I was used to. Instead, she sounded fragile and afraid.

"Of course, Mother," I assured her. "I'll be there today."

Rodney had inherited Daddy's heart disease. I loved Rodney deeply, but we hadn't been close as adults. It was as if we were on different wavelengths. I had always wanted his approval but never felt like I got it. But he was my big brother, and a part of me had always looked up to him.

All the men I loved most in my life had died: Daddy, PaPa, Larry, and now my brother.

~~~~~~~~~~

TWENTY-SIX

River Forest Voicemail

I accepted a position as superintendent of schools in Stoughton, Wisconsin, in 1990. Laura had gone off to college on the East Coast a couple of years earlier, so I was free to go anywhere. When I left Illinois, I hadn't realized how much I'd miss the Lyric Opera, the Ravinia outdoor music festival in Highland Park, and all of the other great things about the city of Chicago. Two years later, I moved back to the area when I became superintendent in River Forest, Illinois.

I came home from work late one night in 1993 and hit the Play button on the answering machine. "Ma'am," a man's voice drawled, "this is Sgt. Barney Hanks, Randolph Air Force Base, Mortuary Division, San Antonio, Texas. Ma'am, I have information about your missing husband, Lt. James L. Hull."

Old feelings of craziness took over. I thought that I'd heard "missing husband," not "dead husband." I pushed the rewind button and hit Play again. The voice repeated, "I have information about your missing husband."

Why had the sergeant said "missing husband?" The question stirred in my brain, buzzing until it exploded into a hopeful voice that screamed, *Maybe he's not dead. Maybe he's alive! What if all this time, he's been alive and you didn't even know?*

Simultaneously, a more rational voice argued, *Tyra, get a grip. You know Larry's dead. You have documents to prove it. They gave you a flag. They only give flags to widows when they know their husbands are dead. You had a memorial service.*

How can you ever be sure? The other part of me countered. *What if there was a mistake? Remember the book in Highland Park? Remember the difference between MIAs and KIAs? He's still not accounted for.*

I put on a pot of coffee then dialed Sgt. Hanks. When I told him who I was, he said, "Ma'am, there's new information. A Vietnamese local turned in human remains. He also found your husband's dog tag in the same area."

I immediately thought that the remains must be Larry's if they were found near the dog tag. I already had his other dog tag. Rescuers had taken it from his neck when they'd tried to retrieve his body.

Sgt. Hanks explained that Larry's plane had gone down approximately five hundred yards inside the Laotian border. The air force also had an aircraft part engraved with the same VIN as Larry's plane. A multinational investigation team would go to the site to determine if there was evidence that it was Larry's crash site. If so, a team would be deployed to excavate the site. If the remains were Larry's, perhaps we could finally have closure. "Ma'am, it could take months to investigate the authenticity of this claim," Sgt. Hanks warned before we hung up.

It was difficult for me to believe Sgt. Hanks's message. I'd been waiting for news for twenty-two years. The phone call ripped away the thin scab on a permanent wound. I asked him to forward me all available documents regarding the recovery by the Vietnamese local. I didn't ask about the possibility that the remains might be someone else's, or whether Larry was perhaps a prisoner of war. As much as I wanted to nurse my briefly resurrected fantasy that Larry might be alive, I wouldn't hang onto it too long. The rational part of me knew it was magical thinking. I didn't want it to get out of hand and make me crazy.

Every time I received information about Larry over the years, I put on one of my favorite songs, "Bridge Over Troubled Water" by Simon and Garfunkel. I'd first heard it when I was in the psychiatric ward in Lubbock after Larry had gone to Vietnam. Larry had been my bridge over troubled water since we'd first met. He was the love of my life—that was my only consolation for losing him so early. Although he had volunteered to go to Nam, I felt as if he had remained emotionally present for me all these years.

With the music playing in the background, I dug in the closet for his battered, old olive Samsonite suitcase. He had rescued it from a dumpster when he worked as a stock boy at the telephone company after we were married. It had become the warehouse for all the documents regarding his death, containing letters of condolence from President Nixon, Senator John Tower from Texas, and the chaplain in Da Nang, along with the official "I regret to inform you" letter and his medals.

I retrieved the suitcase from the back of the closet and rifled through its contents, looking for the last correspondence from Archer Battista. When I called him the next day, he warned me emphatically to be cautious about getting my hopes up about the recovered remains. Locals frequently turned over all sorts of skeletal remains, even animal bones, to officials, hoping to be paid. Then he told me there was someone I should talk to. Colonel Tom Yarborough had been Larry's flight trainer in Vietnam. He had concrete details about how Larry had died. Archer would give the colonel my phone number if that was okay with me. I hung up numb but hopeful. What would the colonel say? No matter what he told me, it would be a relief to know what had really happened to Larry.

Within days, Colonel Yarborough called me. He explained that Larry had been in a Special Forces unit called "Prairie Fire" that had worked in concert with an Army Special Forces unit.

"Tyra, I know exactly what happened to Larry's plane," Colonel Yarborough said. "I've written a book called *Da Nang Diary* about our work there. If you want, I'll send you a copy. But after you read it, you may never want to speak to me again."

"Of course I'll want to speak to you again!" I was adamant. "Why wouldn't I?"

"I'll send you the book. You read it," he instructed. "The chapter titled 'February: Valley of the Shadow of Death' tells in detail how Larry was killed." He paused then said, "And how his plane was destroyed. Call me if you want to talk after you've read it."

The colonel asked about Laura. Larry had bragged to him about our little girl. I'd be sure to tell Laura. Before Tom and I said goodbye, I insisted that no matter what the book said, I'd call back.

I didn't have the patience to wait for Tom's book to arrive. The next day, I went to Barbara's Bookstore in Oak Park to purchase a copy, but they didn't have one in stock. The clerk who ordered it for me said it would be in by the end of the week.

On Friday afternoon, I got the call. Tom's book was waiting for me at the bookstore. I left the office immediately. Anxious to read it, I sat down and turned to the index. Larry's name had several entries next to it. As I flipped through the book, his name jumped out at me from a number of pages. Tom described him as "boyish." I imagined Larry the same way I always saw him: blond hair, blue eyes, and an ear-to-ear grin. Tom was correct—Larry was youthfully good looking. Some Special Forces soldiers had nicknamed him "Woodstock" after the Peanuts character and pasted a Woodstock decal on his flight helmet. According to Tom, they'd idolized Larry, partly as warrior and partly as mascot. They'd even written a poem about his first close call, when he'd flown his plane too low, brushing the tops of trees with his right wing and ending up with some tree branches and limbs stuck in the midsection.

The Ballad of Woodstock

*I love to fly the Oscar Deuce from Channel
one-oh-three.*
 *I fly that dog through rain and fog in the
extreme western DMZ,*
 *And no one knows we're fighting there 'cept
Charlie, you, and me.*
 *So mark my words and heed them well, or
you could end up like me.*
 *I flew down low and got too slow and hit a
goddamn tree!*

I smiled, touched and overwhelmed with gratitude, as I read about the razzing he received from some of the Special Forces guys. *Larry was with men who cared about him,* I consoled myself.

I scanned each page, anxiously looking for Larry's name. I took time to savor each detail Tom wrote about him. I knew what was coming, and I lingered over everything I read about Larry and the men he'd worked beside.

Then there it was, in the chapter Tom had told me about: the description of how Larry had been killed on a special mission over Laos, flying a Forward Air Controller (FAC), a small Cessna that sometimes flew as low as just fifty feet above the treetops.

Several pages into the chapter, he was still in the air. I felt a thrill of relief, despite knowing how the chapter would inevitably end. I flipped through a few more pages. Then came Tom's warning to Larry to watch out for a machine gun on the ridge, while he provided intense air cover for the Bright Light Team, a special forces team dedicated to recovering POWs or downed US pilots in Laos, Cambodia, or North Vietnam. My heart clutched. *Larry, turn back!* I screamed silently. *Please go back! Remember the machine gun on the side of the hill. Remember what Tom told you!*

Four lines further down the page, Tom got a call from the Mobile Launch Team. The Bright Light Team had relayed back to them: Larry's O-2 had been seriously hit by machine gun fire from the ridge and spun out of control to the northwest. They were unable to verify any emergency beepers, indicating there were no survivors.

No, not just like that! I shrieked to myself silently. I flipped frantically back through the pages I'd just read, looking for what I had missed. *How could Larry be dead so fast? How could I lose the love of my life in just four lines?*

Tom flew over Larry's crash site and confirmed its location in a meadow in the A Shau Valley. He stood by until helicopters arrived with a Bright Light Team of twelve men. They found the damage worse than it had first appeared from above. While they were able to remove Sergeant First Class William Fernandez, they couldn't rescue Larry's body from the Cessna wreckage.

I reread the last few pages several times. No matter how many times I read it, it was the same. Larry was dead and had been for twenty-two years.

As I lived Larry's plane crash through Tom's words, I found myself wondering why I was praying for something different to happen even though I already knew the outcome. How could I do that after twenty-two years? I had no answers, only tears. Larry was dead, but I couldn't accept it. For me, it wasn't over.

Larry's body had been left sitting in the cockpit of his plane in the A Shau Valley. Four days later, on February 23, Tom flew to the crash site to say a final good-bye to Larry. As he circled the meadow, he watched in horror as North Vietnamese soldiers scurried beneath the aircraft's wing. I thought of buzzards swooping down to pick the last bits of flesh from the carcasses of cattle, rabbits, or turtles on the highway or in the barren fields of West Texas. Tom described his fury at the thought of what the enemy soldiers might be up to, and I grew furious as I read, too. He told the pilots about seeing the enemy at the site of Larry's downed plane. He recounted his call requesting two Cobra gunships from Quang Tri to attack the NVA soldiers around the crash site. Reading this passage, I recognized my selfishness in assuming that the pilots would try to retrieve Larry's body at all costs. Their purpose was to destroy the enemy.

Tom wrote that it was hazy and smoky because Laotian farmers were burning off their rice fields in an age-old practice. At times, it was almost impossible to see the downed Cessna O-2 below. Tom tried to verbally mark the target next to Larry's plane for the Cobra pilots, but due to the haze and smoke it was impossible for them to locate their target. In frustration after three failed attempts, Tom fired a smoke rocket near Larry's right wing to mark the spot for the Cobras. As he fired and dipped his wing to release the rocket, he inadvertently hit the center of Larry's right wing. In seconds, Larry's plane was engulfed in an orange ball of flame and black smoke, a funeral pyre with Larry still sitting at the controls. As the Cobras radioed their condolences, Tom described moving the control stick mechanically through an aileron roll over what he thought was Larry's final resting place.

Tom's error was catastrophic. I recalled the lore about the Vikings, who put fallen warriors out to sea in burning boats so the smoke from the funeral pyre could carry their souls to Valhalla, and I felt comforted somehow by what Tom had inadvertently done.

Tom had told me I might never want to speak to him again. My reaction was the opposite. I wanted to meet him, and I wanted Laura to meet him. I wanted Tom to tell her what kind of a man her father was, not just as a pilot. I wanted him to tell her about Larry's kindness, sense of humor, compassion, and honor. I wanted to write Tom, but I wasn't sure what to say. I decided on the truth: how I'd felt when I read that he'd inadvertently burned Larry's plane.

I reread Tom's pages over and over, weeping silently in the bookstore. Time seemed to halt, the way it does when you go somewhere in your mind. When I finally looked down at my watch, it was late. I had a big night ahead of me. I was hosting a party for my school board, the administrators, and their spouses. My mother had even flown into town to join us. I went home and showed Mother Tom's book. She wept as she read.

Although going to the party was the last thing I felt like doing, it was too late to cancel. Besides, I could hear Larry's voice in my ear, *Girl, you know it's all gonna be all right. It came to pass, didn't it? Like the Bible says, it came to pass. Let it pass on through. You wanted to know what happened. Now you know. You've got work to do.*

"Mother, tonight we're going to look right and act right," I declared, as much to keep myself going as to encourage her. "We need to get dressed. I'm hosting a party." Throughout the party, I heard Larry telling me to buck up whenever I felt teary-eyed and overwhelmed. I stood proud and did my best to make our new administrators and their spouses feel at home. When it was over, I was glad I hadn't canceled the evening. Afterward, Larry filled my thoughts again. Had he known he was going to crash? Had he tried to land his plane? Had he been killed instantly?

I tried to make sense of the disparate information I had: Tom's account of destroying Larry's plane while his body was still in the cockpit and Sergeant Hanks' claim of recovered human remains, Larry's dog tag, and plane part. Overcome by years of not knowing what had happened, my heart ached to know the truth. Some of Larry's remains might still be in Laos. Some of his bones might be in the hands of American authorities. Before he'd left for Vietnam, he had asked to be buried at Arlington if anything happened to him. I had promised to do so.

Would I ever be able to keep that promise?

TWENTY-SEVEN

The Vietnam Memorial, Washington, DC

Even though Sergeant Hanks warned me it could take months or even years to close Larry's case, and Archer and Tom had both cautioned me about the black market for US soldiers' dog tags and remains, I was elated. The phone call I received in 1993 resurrected my hope that Larry's remains would be found and returned to us. Over the twenty-two years since his death, my frame of mind had vacillated between, *Give it up, Tyra, you don't have a prayer*, and, *God, please bring Larry home so I can keep my promise to bury him at Arlington.*

Sergeant Hanks' call was the first time we'd received concrete information regarding the probable location of Larry's crash site. On good days, I believed deep in my soul that the remains discovered by the Vietnamese turtle farmer were Larry's because they'd been found next to his dog tag. Larry always wore his dog tags. Whenever I pictured him, I saw them dangling around his neck. The dog tags and Larry belonged together, and I felt confident we'd bring him home soon. Though it may sound like wishful thinking, I believed.

The Monday after Sergeant Hanks called, I told Aaron, my school board president and a social worker, about the circumstances of Larry's death and Tom's book. I hoped I might receive a phone call any day that Larry was coming home, and I'd need to take off work to make arrangements for his funeral at Arlington.

I told Aaron so he wouldn't be blindsided. I also trusted him, and I needed to tell someone.

Later that day, Aaron phoned to tell me he had purchased *Da Nang Diary* and had already begun to read it. I no longer felt so alone in my ceaseless hoping and praying for Larry to find his way home. I had Sergeant Hanks, Tom, Archer, and now Aaron, who understood. I called Tom almost every time I received an official letter or a call with information about Larry. I gave the air force my office address and phone number so they could reach me during the day. On nights when I found important messages waiting on the voicemail machine at home, I couldn't call back until the next day and spent sleepless nights fantasizing about Larry's remains lying somewhere in the jungle.

The calls and letters started to drag me down. Positive news cracked open the cache of grief in my heart, shedding rays of hope and light on our situation. Work was my salvation. It soothed my soul, and I lost myself in my job on behalf of the children, the teachers, and the district.

Tom, Archer, and I made plans to gather in Washington, DC, for a Memorial Day weekend visit to The Wall in May of 1994. After seeing The Moving Wall in Chicago at the Vietnam Veterans Homecoming Parade, I had promised to take Laura to Washington to see the permanent installation. But I'd felt a sense of foreboding and hadn't had the courage to fly with her to Washington, just the two of us. I knew Larry was dead, but my emotions did my own version of the Texas two-step when I considered going to DC—one step forward, two steps back. I couldn't understand or articulate my fear, other than wondering if there was a part of me that wanted to keep the hope intact that Larry might not be dead, instead of accepting that he was truly gone and placing my hope in getting his remains back. With the exception of The Moving Wall, I had never been to a monument where Larry's name was inscribed in a place of honor. Seeing his name on the official wall would be a formal and permanent confirmation of his death.

With Tom escorting us to the Vietnam Memorial, I knew we'd be okay. I looked forward to meeting him, someone who had loved Larry, fought with him, and was the last to see his body in the cockpit of his plane. Other than Archer, I knew no one else who had been with Larry the last eight months of his life. Laura and I invited Mother and Larry's family to join us. I was sad when the Hulls decided not to go. I often thought that in her unbearable grief, Larry's mother believed he would surprise us all one day and walk out of the jungle. Her heart was as broken as mine.

My nerves twittered as our plane circled over the airport, preparing for landing in DC, and I spotted the Washington Monument and reflection pool and The Wall below. It was my first visit to Washington, and my heart was filled with anticipation and dread. The Capitol was teeming with people in town for Memorial Day weekend.

I was unsure how I felt about meeting Tom for the first time and about going to The Wall. I was driven to do both, but my emotions were mixed. Filled with excitement and anticipation one minute, the next, I felt like running away from it all. I couldn't describe the contradictory feelings rumbling in my gut except that it felt as if a volcano was on the verge of erupting. I knew once I saw Larry's name on The Wall, I could never pretend it didn't belong there. Instead of admitting this to Laura, I talked about how much I appreciated Tom for offering to escort us to see it.

The next morning, we waited for Tom in the hotel lobby. He had told me he'd be wearing a blue suit, and I had a picture of him in my mind based on his photo on the back cover of *Da Nang Diary*. We waited for him at the foot of the escalator. I looked up and immediately recognized him. "He's here," I said, as he stepped off the escalator. Despite how much we'd shared over the phone and in writing, it felt a bit awkward now that we were finally meeting in person. I reminded myself that Tom was a compatriot of Larry's and relaxed. We were in good hands.

We began at one end of The Wall, where a book of names was located. Tom knew where Larry's name was, but he wanted us to know how to look it up. Names of our fallen heroes are listed alphabetically in each of the books located at either end of The Wall. We found Larry's address, Panel 05 W, Row 120. The dull etched letters stood out, their edges glistening from the rays of the sun striking The Wall's shiny black finish. Our own reflections sent moving shadows down the wall as we walked toward the center to First Lt. James L. Hull.

Larry's name was located five rows from the bottom. My heart sank. It was as if we had come home to Larry. It was the closest I'd felt to him physically since he deployed to Vietnam. I felt closer to Larry than I had at the cemetery where we'd had his memorial service. It wasn't Arlington National Cemetery, but it was the best we had. It was the first time Laura and I were together at a place that honored her father. A park ranger helped Mother make a rubbing of Larry's name as Tom stepped back, respectful of our privacy.

Tom was the perfect escort, knowledgeable and attentive. Knowing he had been with Larry his last days made him seem like a kind of holy ambassador. As we toured the Mall, he answered our questions and offered tidbits of information about Larry he thought we would find interesting. We strolled through the park, where the loud thunder of thousands of motorcycles driven by the Rolling Thunder Brigade, an advocacy group dedicated to bringing a full accounting of POWs and MIAs from all past wars, especially Vietnam, drowned out our conversation.

At the end of the day, Tom drove us back to the hotel. Laura, Mother, and I were exhausted, partly from walking around the Mall but also from all the emotions the visit had brought.

Once we were back in our room, Laura said, "Mom, Tom doesn't like me."

"That's not true," I countered. "He was so thrilled to finally meet you and has talked about how he had wanted to look you up all these years. You're the most special one here," I assured her. "What makes you think Tom doesn't like you?"

"He won't look at me. He looks away when he talks to me. He doesn't look in my eyes." I could hear the pain in her words, and I felt badly that she believed this.

"I know Tom wants to be close to us. He's especially drawn to you since he was so close to Larry, and you're Larry's daughter," I assured her.

Laura looked unconvinced but didn't say anything more. We both laid down to rest before dinner.

We rode with Tom, Archer, and their wives to dinner at the Willard Hotel. Presidents, politicians, and other famous personalities had dined there since the 1800s, and some of their photos adorned the walls. I sat at the head of the table, with Laura to my right and Tom on my left, facing her. We were barely seated when Tom said, "Laura, I want to apologize to you. It's hard for me to look at you. Looking into your eyes is just like looking at Larry."

Caught off guard, I turned to Laura. Her eyes were soft. "I knew something was wrong," she answered. "I told Mother after we got back from The Wall I didn't think you liked me because you wouldn't look at me. I feel better now that I know the reason.

"When I was in third grade, Mother freaked out the first time she saw me write my name in cursive. She said my handwriting was exactly like my father's. That's a good thing, huh?" Laura smiled.

Relief wafted over the group, cleansing all of us of any discomfort or self-consciousness. The evening was filled with conversation about Larry and the war, including discussions about what we'd all been up to the past twenty-two years. Tom and Archer were especially interested in Laura. Occasionally, one of us would touch on the possibility of Larry's remains coming home. Both Tom and Archer were reluctant to expect it, though it felt like their reluctance was in large part to protect Laura or me from getting our hopes up too much.

The evening ended too soon. As we said good-bye to them in front of the hotel, we promised to stay in touch and keep one another apprised of any information we heard relating to Larry.

Mother, Laura, and I attended the Memorial Day concert the next day on the Capitol grounds with my sister-in-law and her family, who were also in DC for the holiday weekend. Laura and I decided to take a cab back over to The Wall afterward. She reached over in the cab and squeezed my hand. The cabbie told us night-time was great for seeing The Wall. "It changes its personality throughout the night each time the light on it shifts," he explained.

He was correct. It was a totally different experience at night. I looked up at the moon and told Laura the story of when she was a baby and we were all in Florida for Larry's training on the O-2 before he deployed to Vietnam.

"Your Daddy once told me, 'Whenever you miss me, look up and know I'm looking at the same moon.'" I put my arm around Laura's waist.

"He loved it when you buried his feet in the sand when we went to the beach. You'd squeal with delight when he wiggled his toes to make the sand fall off. You'd hurry to pile more on, and he'd wiggle it off again. You two did it over and over, and we all laughed 'til we cried."

"I wish I could remember him," she whispered as we stood in front of Larry's name on The Wall. It felt holy, sacred, and precious to be there—the three of us finally together again.

TWENTY-EIGHT

A DNA Match

After the 1993 phone call, the Joint Task Force Full Accounting Command recommended a follow-up investigation of Larry's crash site. Over the next ten years, I received approximately
twenty-two letters specific to Larry's case, along with Department of Defense POW/MIA newsletters, next-of-kin letters,
newsletters published by the Office of the Assistant Secretary of
Defense, and news regarding the National League of POW/MIA
Families' annual conferences.

Just as I kept documentation on Larry in his old suitcase, I'd
learned to file all my unanswered questions—and the hopes ignited
by each new report from the Command—in a special box on an
imaginary shelf in my mind. When too much time passed for my
comfort level, I'd call or write the Mortuary Division at Randolph
Air Force Base in San Antonio, Texas, and ask for specific details
on the next scheduled excavation attempt. Sometimes, excavations
were called off due to weather conditions. Other times, they were
canceled or never scheduled due to political issues, or because of
the lack of a safe landing zone in the vicinity of the crash site.

Meanwhile, life moved on. Laura was living in Madison, Wisconsin, where she worked in the food industry and completed
a technology degree. I continued to enjoy my work as superintendent of schools and was proud of my accomplishments. The
River Forest faculty was committed to offering the best possible

opportunities for our students, and we worked tirelessly. It was an educator's dream.

I was invited to serve as a trustee on the board of the Family Service and Mental Health Center of Oak Park and River Forest. It was thrilling for me to serve children and their families through counseling and educational programs, as well as adult clients who participated in a day treatment program. My life was full and good, except for my unfinished business with Larry.

In July 1997, I learned Larry's was one of seventy-one cases scheduled for excavation in Laos. A letter explained that thirty excavations were scheduled for each year. A trilateral excavation team made up of Vietnamese, Laotian, and American members would go in once the Laotian government granted permission. Crash site investigations began in the northern part of Laos and would work down in a southerly direction. Larry's crash site was believed to be in the Xekong Province in Laos, two provinces south of where excavations were going on at that time. It was unknown when his crash site would be investigated. In other words, I read the letter to mean, "Don't get your hopes up, Tyra."

We've been here before, I thought to myself. *Someday, Larry, you'll come home*, I promised. *I'm not giving up.*

In 2001, authorities finally confirmed that the skeletal remains found by the Vietnamese turtle farmer in Laos in 1993 matched Larry's mother's DNA. Mrs. Hull was very ill, but she and his dad had both lived long enough to hear this wonderful news. I was elated. My hope that I could keep the promise I had made to bury Larry at Arlington National Cemetery grew stronger. But the remains would stay at the joint POW/MIA Accounting Command (JPAC) in Hawaii until the Laotian crash site could be fully excavated and Larry's case closed. Since there was no date set for excavating the crash site yet, I had to remind myself that it could be months or years until we had a full resolution.

I retired in 2004 from my position as superintendent of schools in River Forest after thirty-two years in the public school business. Laura had moved to Chicago and was working for a technology company. I accepted a position at Dominican University in River Forest, teaching graduate students in the school administration program, and later as the Director of the Master of Arts in Teaching Program.

I'd begun writing chapters for this book in 1984. After I retired, I had more time to write. I frequently woke up during the night wondering how I would end it. I dreaded the thought of publishing our story before Larry's remains were returned.

On July 26, 2006, I walked to my car after teaching an evening class. I'd missed a call on my cell phone from a phone number I didn't recognize. I slid into the driver's seat of my car, put the window down, and returned the call.

When Nat Hernandez answered, I recognized his voice before he said his name. He was one of the men I spoke with on a regular basis at the Mortuary Division at Randolph Air Force Base about the status of Larry's crash site excavation.

Nat lost no time giving me the news. "Dr. Manning, Lieutenant Hull's site has been excavated. His case is closed." I sat frozen in my car. "His case is closed," Nat reiterated.

"Nat, say that again. Please say it again." I could barely get the words out. My throat was dry, my chest tight, as a paralyzing sensation moved from the top of my skull down my torso.

"Dr. Manning, it's true. Lieutenant Hull's crash site has been excavated. His case is closed." Nat's voice brimmed with excitement. "We would like to set up a time to meet with you and your daughter to go over the findings at the crash site, as well as the forensic evidence. Once you've read and signed off on the documents, we can plan Larry's funeral at Arlington."

Larry was coming home.

I had imagined this day thousands of times in my dreams, especially in the early mornings, when the line between sleeping and waking blurred. But in the stark reality of the university parking lot, it was difficult to imagine that it was really happening.

It was too late to call Laura; she'd told me she'd stayed up late the night before finishing a work project and was going to bed early tonight. *I want to go home and be with Larry*, I thought. *I'll sit on the front porch and in my mind's eye I'll go there—to the beach, where the water meets the sand. I'll go there and tell Larry, We're coming for you. Just like I promised, Larry. We're coming to bring you home.*

That night, I sat on the porch looking at the stars and imagining the rest of Larry's remains coming home from the jungle. His 1993 bones were at Hickam Air Force Base in Hawaii. Now, the last of his remains had been excavated and removed from Laos.

Foremost in my mind was keeping my promise that Larry be buried at Arlington. But since 1993, I had also struggled with knowing that Larry's crash site had been disturbed and that his remains were only partially recovered. Before 1993, I had imagined him all in one place in the jungle. After 1993, I was grateful that some of his remains had been found and were returned to JPAC, but it was unsettling that they had been separated from the site before it could be completely excavated and all of his remains recovered. I felt a haunting insistence that all of Larry be in one place. This feeling became more intense after his 1993 remains were moved. It didn't feel holy or respectful for him to be spread all over the place.

The next day, I waited until Laura got off work before I stopped by her condominium to tell her about Larry. Reluctant to believe it was finally over, Laura begged me to be cautious about thinking we were really going to escort him home to Arlington until Nat and his partner presented the forensic proof and details of the final excavation of the crash site.

They arrived at my house in late September. I felt relieved when Nat introduced himself. It was like meeting a long-lost relative. We'd talked about Larry's case so many times over the years. Laura was running late. I made coffee, and the three of us discussed their flight to Chicago, my career in education, Nat's children, and his partner's plans to retire soon. Laura still hadn't arrived, so I called her cell phone.

"Where are you?" I asked when she answered. "They're here."

The line was silent.

"Laura," I said. "Are you all right?"

"Mom, I . . . I've started my car twice and then needed to go back and see if I remembered to lock the doors and make sure the stove was turned off. I'm getting ready to leave again. I should be there in about forty-five minutes."

I sheepishly said to Nat and his partner, "Laura hasn't left yet, but she's on her way now. I think maybe she's a little nervous about our meeting. She wasn't quite two years old when her father was killed, and she's thirty-seven now," I explained.

"It's not a problem. This is all we have to do today." Nat said. He was very gracious and understanding.

Laura called several more times. She finally said, "Mother, I'm having a hard time getting there. I don't know why, but I am."

When she finally arrived three hours later, she appeared calm and steady. Soon after, Nat and his companion began their presentation. Laura worked out her discomfort and anxiety by listening quietly, just like her father. I demonstrated mine by talking, talking, talking. We got through the forensic data and documentation of the match between the recovered bones and Mrs. Hull's DNA sample, and the file of activity related to Larry's case from 1971 through 2006.

We planned Larry's funeral at Arlington for November 13. Laura and I looked at casket options and chose mahogany. Nat explained it would be a funeral with full military honors. I was thrilled Larry was getting all that he deserved.

As we worked out the details, I remember thinking that even though Larry had died in 1971, his memorial service had felt like we were all pretending, since his body hadn't been there. This time felt much more real. Larry might have died thirty-five years earlier, but now we were choosing a casket; we were going to Hawaii to bring him home to a real grave at Arlington. Sadly, both Larry's parents had passed away several years earlier.

By the time we finished making our decisions, we had gone through countless pots of coffee, and Laura and I were numb with grief and gratitude. In some ways, I felt as if Larry had just died and the last thirty-five years hadn't happened. When I had those feelings, I looked at Laura, now twelve years older than her father had been when his plane crashed. Time had passed—and life had been rich and full with so much goodness. Laura and I had both grown up in so many ways. Now, I had the ending to the love story between Larry and me.

TWENTY-NINE

Bringing Larry Home

On November 8, 2006, Laura and I flew to Hawaii to accept Larry's remains and escort them to Washington, DC. He would soon be buried at Arlington. The next morning, we met Doyle, our air force escort, in the Hale Koa Hotel, which served active and retired military families. He and Nat had created our itinerary. Organized and gracious, Doyle appeared to be about my age. He had reddish-gray hair and blue eyes and would be with us throughout our entire journey. He suggested we have breakfast in the hotel before we drove to JPAC, where we would meet with officials and accept Larry's remains. He would not leave us until Larry's funeral was over. As a superintendent, I had always been in charge, but in this, I let Doyle, Laura, and the universe be responsible for our plans. I wanted to savor every moment.

As Laura and I stepped through the doors of JPAC on Hickam Air Force Base in Honolulu, the deputy commander greeted us and invited us to take a photograph in front of the large wall, named Operation Homecoming Commemorative, 1973–Present. It listed the names of recovered POWs/MIAs representing all branches of our country's armed services since 1973. Larry's name would soon be added. Doyle, Laura, and I followed the deputy commander through locked doors, down a hallway into a conference room. I noticed the nametags on the table, denoting our assigned seats. I had sat around similar oval tables in boardrooms throughout my career. As "Dr. Manning," I had always felt confident and sure of myself. I reached deep down now to grasp that self-assurance. Instead, I touched the soul of my twenty-four-year-old self, the frightened and unsteady young woman I had been when Larry died. I trembled with raw emotion at the thought of seeing his physical remains. I feared that if I did not see and touch his bones, I would not be able to say good-bye.

As soon as we took our seats, I asked about Larry's missing dog tag. A young anthropologist assigned to Larry's case seemed uncomfortable and embarrassed. He explained that once they had received the dog tag and other remains from the Vietnamese turtle farmer, American authorities had been required to turn the dog tag over to South Vietnamese officials. Since then, it had gone missing.

"The good news," he offered, "is that while it was in our possession we took a photograph."

I have always hated incomplete pairs—missing chessmen, a lost salt or peppershaker, one dog tag from my missing husband's matched set. I thought of the dog tag I'd had since Larry's death as the 1971 dog tag. Larry's comrades had ripped it from his neck while trying to recover his body after his plane crashed. I desperately wanted the pair of dog tags that had dangled on the chain around Larry's neck, just below the knitted rib of his T-shirt. I reminded myself that today I would get to see Larry's remains, which muted some of my disappointment. A photo would have to suffice.

We were not the only ones who had waited for this day to arrive. The team of professionals assigned to Larry's thirty-five-year-old case impressed Laura and me with their personal knowledge of him and us. They were experts and knew all the details regarding the search efforts for Larry's remains. The anthropologist's voice softened, and he spoke from a place of personal disappointment as he described the difficulty they had encountered trying to negotiate permission to excavate Larry's crash site in 1993.

We were invited to tour the facility, and as we worked our way down the hall, we stopped to observe lab technicians in white coats working at small tables holding skeletal remains and other material evidence. Further down, we were introduced to a young woman sitting on a high stool in front of an oversized computer screen. She explained that she was examining DNA samples for identification purposes. I thanked her for her work and explained that the comparison of Larry's mother's DNA to his remains had been immeasurably valuable to Laura and me, giving us the comfort that Larry had truly been found. Each time Laura and I were introduced to one of the staff as Lt. Hull's family, immediate recognition of Larry's name flashed across their faces. They had not forgotten First Lieutenant James Larry Hull. I was instantly grateful, and it made me proud to be an American. Larry would have expected nothing less from his country. Guilty of losing faith over the years, I whispered a private apology.

When we returned to the conference room, an olive-green blanket lay lengthwise down the center of the table. Doyle told us that Larry's remains were inside. I went numb. I gripped Laura's arm tight. "Larry was a young, proud first lieutenant in the blue United States Air Force. Couldn't you find a blue blanket for him?" I couldn't help asking.

After a long silence, the Deputy Commander said, "Dr. Manning, it's military issue. Every branch of the armed forces uses an olive-green military blanket. There's one exception: The Navy uses a white blanket."

Assured by his explanation, I turned to Laura. "I want us to be alone."

The deputy commander, his assistant, the anthropologist, and Doyle left the room. I heard one of them tell Laura they would be right outside if we needed them. When the door closed, Laura stepped to my side. "Momma, I'll be right behind you," she whispered. Then she moved back and stood against the wall.

Finally, I was alone with my husband. I placed my hands on the table. A deep guttural sound erupted from me. Tears streamed as I moved my hands onto the wool blanket. Lightly and gently, with palms wide open, I pressed down until I felt the solid hardness of bones.

Larry.

"Tell them I want them to unwrap the blanket."

"Are you sure, Mother?" Laura asked. My mind reeled back to 1971, when I'd first learned Larry was dead. My nine-year-old self had saved me then. Today, Larry's and my daughter was there if I needed her.

"Yes. Is it okay with you, or do you want to leave?"

"I'm fine either way. I'll get them." Laura moved to the door.

The entire group stepped back into the conference room. Doyle moved to the table and gently undid each safety pin holding Larry's bones secure inside. Then he gently unfolded and spread the top of the blanket onto the table, leaving Larry's bones visible but still snug in the blanket.

When Daddy died, I had moved a stool up to his casket, stood on it, and kissed him good-bye. Now I stood facing Larry's bones, encased in plastic bags. I laid my hands on the remnants of my husband. An electric charge vibrated through my body and up my spine. I saw him there in front of me, grinning from ear to ear, his blue eyes sparkling, his blond hair shining, both dog tags hanging around his neck.

"I slept with these bones," I turned and said to Laura. "These are your father's."

Laura moved beside me and put her arm around my waist. "Are you ready, Mother?"

Our tears mingled as we hugged, and I nodded yes.

A somber young man in a lab coat assisted me as I painstakingly rewrapped the blanket around Larry's bones and safety pinned it closed. The funeral home aides gently placed the blanket on a gurney and wheeled Larry to their vehicle to be transported to the funeral home.

During the ride to the funeral home to view the casket, Laura and I carefully examined the artifacts that JPAC had excavated at Larry's crash site. The reality of the years that had passed stunned me as I studied the artifacts that had lain with Larry in the jungle. How could thirty-five years have gone by already? *Because the universe doesn't stop the clock until your personal mysteries are resolved,* I murmured to myself. Our daughter was sitting next to me. She was thirty-seven years old. Her father had been twenty-five when he was killed. I was now fifty-nine but felt twenty-four. More than half my life had passed since Larry died. Past and future realities moved in and out of the present.

A mission code card encased in plastic demanded my attention. I had watched Larry strap a similar rectangular plastic protective sleeve just above his knee with a Velcro band every morning before he left for work, on his way to the flight line during pilot training. It held necessary documents such as maps and mission cards. In my mind's eye, at that very moment, Larry was standing by the kitchen door, grinning and handsome in his flight suit and sunglasses, the flight card strapped onto his leg. I saw the slightest twinge of machismo in him only when he was suited up to fly. My heart smiled a secret smile.

Along with the mission code card, there were two fragments of sunglass lenses, a US government-issue Skilcraft ballpoint pen casing, and what the identification list described as a "probable watchband buckle." Laura and I had postponed one decision: What should we do with the artifacts, officially known as evidence, found with Larry's remains at the excavation site in Laos?

We were still going through the artifacts when Doyle announced we were lost. He turned the rental car onto a side street, parked, and placed a call for directions.

"For God's sake, I'm not going to lose Larry again!" I quipped.

Once we found the funeral home, we followed Doyle into the small parlor. I knew how to do funerals. The ritual began with the acceptance that someone had died. This time, it was Larry. It would end when we went to the grave and Larry was lowered into the ground.

I asked Laura to tell Doyle to please give us some privacy. Doyle assured us he would be just outside the door as he gently closed it behind him.

Then Laura and I were alone with Larry one last time.

Larry's uniform, complete with his First Lieutenant bars, name, wings, and the medals he had earned, lay in the casket on top of his bones, demonstrating without a doubt that First Lieutenant James Larry Hull was ready to be buried. Laura and I held each other. I put my hand inside the casket. I could feel the blanket. I pressed harder with my hand until I felt the unyielding bones again. They were there. The only things missing were the artifacts. Laura and I held each one, bagged in plastic. They had lain with Larry in the Laotian soil since his plane crashed in 1971. To us, they had become relics: precious, honorable, and holy. We placed them one by one beneath Larry's blanket with his bones.

We were taking Larry to Washington, DC, where he would be buried at Arlington in his final resting place. Laura couldn't remember her father's first memorial service, but I did. A floral arrangement had sat in the front of my hometown church in place of a casket. It was the best I could do at the time, but I'd never quit believing that one day Larry would come home and I'd keep my promise. We were going to Arlington for a real funeral for Larry. This time, he would have a real casket.

Before we left the funeral home I walked over to the closed casket and tried lifting the top. It was locked tight. Laura put her hand over my arm as we stepped away. We would not see the casket again until tomorrow, when we boarded the plane back to the mainland. As Laura and I stepped out of the room, I glanced back for one more reassuring look at the casket. It was still there.

THIRTY

After the Funeral Home

We returned to the hotel. Laura said she was exhausted and headed back to our room for a nap. I was drawn to the beach. I walked, and then ran, to where the sand and the water met. Finding Larry was the goal. I rounded the corner of the building then raced to the water, pulling off my heels and knee-high stockings as I ran. With my pant legs rolled almost to my knees, I waded in as the surf splashed over the tops of my feet. Water sprayed up my legs, soaking my pants. Planting my feet wide enough apart to prevent me from falling from the sudden force of the surf, I waited.

Larry wasn't there.

I calmed myself, breathed deeply, closed my eyes, and then opened them again. I was looking for Larry, as if I expected him to walk toward me.

No Larry.

I had touched him just a few hours ago, laid my hands on his bones, and pressed hard. Flesh to bone, just as I had wrapped my arms around his neck, pressing and hugging him in the airport parking lot in Lubbock in 1970.

I sobbed violently, without making a sound. I knew without a doubt that Larry was dead. But reality was blurred by all the plans and dreams we'd had of meeting for R&R on the beach in Hawaii, which, by some marvelous ironic miracle, was where I was now. A part of me had expected Larry to meet me there. I longed to hold him one more time, to connect with him spiritually in my mind and to be with him in human, physical form. Now, the fantasy that I would be with him one more time was over.

Devastated, I waded back through the waist-high waves, tumbled into a beach chair not far from the water's edge, and relived our time at JPAC earlier in the day. I had always thought my obsession with Larry's remains coming home was because I had promised him he would be buried at Arlington. But when I touched his bones at JPAC, I'd realized they were holy. I *had* held Larry one last time. My husband would never physically walk down the beach to meet me. I accepted that. His remains were all I had left of his precious body, the vessel that had housed his spirit. Their recovery brought me immeasurable peace. What I discovered that day was that humans have a primal need to honor not just the spirit and soul of the deceased but also the container—the body that held them. And I knew in my heart that Larry would still meet me at the beach in my mind's eye, whenever I needed him. Flesh and bones die, but loving relationships never do.

In 1971, when I was at the Clinic and first learned Larry was dead, I'd pushed the Rewind button over and over again on the cassette tapes Larry had made me, He'd talked about the plans we'd made to meet each other for R&R on the beach in Hawaii. Now here I was, on that same beach. It was hard to grasp. Past dreams and plans slammed into the present, leaving me stunned and unsure of reality.

Teary and exhausted, I left the beach, stopping at an outdoor coffee bar overlooking the ocean. As I sat in a chair in front of the café, sipping and staring blindly into the bright green foliage around me, my eyes focused on shocking pink blossoms adorned with strong, full petals. Their beauty spoke to me: *The universe is in order. Focus on the miracle. Larry is home. He's going to Arlington just as he wanted, just as you promised. Don't lose this miracle to tears and sadness. Feel the sun. Feel the warmth.* I'd gotten what I had prayed for, a time to honor and celebrate my husband, Laura's daddy—the man who had come home in the evenings after flight training and tossed his baby girl gently into the air, caught her, and blew bubbles on her tummy until she screamed in laughter. This was my Larry, who'd made love to me and sometimes tickled me 'til I cried.

I walked back toward the hotel. It was filled with soldiers on leave from temporary duty assignments in faraway places. Spouses and lovers joined them in Hawaii, the same paradise Larry and I had fantasized about on tapes we had mailed back and forth as we anticipated our second honeymoon on R&R. Larry's plane crash kept our dream from becoming a reality.

Passing by military families on vacation was excruciating. I found myself captivated by a young couple with a baby girl. They could have easily been the First Lieutenant James Larry Hull family. I looked again at the bright pink flowers surrounded by lush green leaves and vines. *Focus on the miracle.* I heard the words in my head again, then Larry's voice chimed in, reiterating the encouraging mantra included in all the cassette tapes he had mailed home to me. "Girl, it's going to be fine. Remember, girl, I love you."

I never wanted to forget this day, where I went and what I did. It seemed as if I should return home having recorded every detail. I wandered aimlessly on the grounds, shooting photos with my cell phone to demonstrate that I had indeed been to paradise. My memory was packed with details of Larry, the JPAC lab, and the funeral home.

Whenever I was worried about something, Larry used to say, "Girl, it will pass. Don't you know? It won't be like this forever. Just do one day at a time. Besides, you got me."

He was right. It had all come to pass. I made a decision right then to be present for every minute of the rest of the journey through burying Larry. It was the only way to ever have it truly over. One promise not kept—to walk with him on the beach—exchanged for another. He would be buried at Arlington National Cemetery.

"Where have you been? Are you okay?" Our lovely Laura looked at me with concern when I opened the hotel room door a little while later. "Let's go for a walk on the beach and find a nice restaurant for dinner," she continued. "I'm not really hungry, but we should try to eat and stay up as late as we can. We're leaving late tomorrow afternoon, and we'll need to sleep on the plane. I can't believe we arrived only yesterday."

"We lived forever today," I said, sighing with exhaustion.

We were sharing a hotel room, and in an effort to be considerate of each other, we tried to keep our belongings picked up and put away. Makeup and toiletries overflowed from the tiny vanity in the bathroom onto the built-in countertop in the small bedroom. Twin beds and a chair left little room to move around. We were cautious as we stepped around suitcases, hanging clothes, and my many pairs of shoes. I'd brought shoes for the beach, shoes for the funeral, and comfortable shoes for walking, outdoing my already notorious reputation for packing too much when traveling.

I was adamant that the programs for Larry's funeral and the guest register for the reception, along with the large folder of materials we'd been given at JPAC—including an eight-by-ten photograph of Laura and me with JPAC personnel and the photograph of Larry's missing dog tag—would only be safe if I carried them. None of these materials could be trusted for travel in baggage cargo and required an additional briefcase, along with my laptop for journaling and emailing. Staying connected to the outside world helped me stay grounded in the present, so I wouldn't get swept away by the past.

There was something else I wanted very badly to carry on the plane with me but couldn't. Larry's remains were to be transported in his casket, which would be placed with the other checked baggage. We had a layover and plane change in Dallas, which meant the cargo would be transported from one plane to the next as well. During dinner that night at an open-air restaurant overlooking the beach, I confided in Laura. "I'm uncomfortable saying this out loud, because it sounds sacrilegious, but . . ."

"What is it, Mother?" Laura encouraged.

"I had a dream. Do you remember the time we had a layover in Dallas and our luggage got lost? We stayed in the hotel at the airport. Do you remember how long it took them to find our bags? Laura, what if they lose your dad in cargo?"

Laura stared at me, speechless. Our nervous giggles grew into louder chuckles and then into belly laughs. It was the kind of laughter that seemed as if it would never stop, laughter that continued into sweet, calm exhaustion. Laura reached over and held my hand as our tears of laughter transformed into tears of relief. Our waiter asked if everything was all right, and we nodded, faces flooded with relieved, happy-sad tears. I gave thanks to God and Larry for our dear Laura.

~~~

Friday, November 10, 2006, was a blur. We packed and then met Doyle for breakfast. Laura had a number of well-thought-out questions regarding the funeral and protocol at the chapel and cemetery. Doyle's answers forced me to acknowledge that we had passed only the first emotional hurdle of this fantastic and, at times, frightening journey. It was frightening because the emotions and grief of losing Larry were no longer chasing me. They were standing right in front of me challenging me with their reality and demanding that I confront them or run back into an old repressive world. But I wouldn't go back there. I didn't even know where or how to run anymore.

I felt confused and scattered, as if my soul was leaking. It was all there: the feelings of a fifty-nine-year-old woman whose husband was being returned thirty-five years after his death and the grief of a twenty-four-year-old, frightened, and clinically depressed young woman. I was carrying the grief that had been locked inside me for thirty-five years through this journey. I vowed to breathe and feel and release it.

Doyle reiterated the day's schedule. We wouldn't need to leave for the airport until 3:00 p.m. for our early evening flight. We'd sleep overnight on the plane and arrive in Dallas around 5:00 a.m. I asked Doyle if I could go down to the runway and observe Larry's casket being boarded onto the plane. It would take special clearance, but he thought it might be arranged.

Laura lightened the somber mood a bit by suggesting we go to Pearl Harbor and the Punch Bowl Memorial. I liked the idea. Over the years, several friends had brought back photographs of Larry's name inscribed on a wall at the Punch Bowl Memorial. We headed for Pearl Harbor first. The real Hawaii was a stark contrast to my fantasies. I marveled at the heavy rush-hour traffic on the island, surprised at its similarity to Chicago.

I was also struck by the similarity of my feelings regarding Larry's death and my father's death. As a child, I had wondered why other people acted as if my daddy had not died, like when Mr. Doncaster took me with him to get his children at the swimming pool and my friends yelled, "Hey, Tyra, are you coming in?" How could I have gone swimming when my father was dead, my whole world changed forever? And how could the world go on now, without even a blip, when Larry's remains were finally home? Yet once again, it was; people around us continued to live their lives. But this time, it felt like a good thing. It meant I had a world to go back to when this was over.

Just before Laura and I left for Hawaii, I had sought out psychiatric counsel. "I'm a fifty-nine-year-old woman crying the tears of a twenty-four-year-old widow," I confided in the doctor. "I see familiar places that remind me of Larry. I think I see him walking down the street, turn my car around, and go back to check if he's there. Larry never lived in Chicago, but I've always felt his energy. I feel him now, stronger than ever. I still go to him in my mind's eye, like I have since he was killed. Am I losing it again?"

The understanding psychiatrist listened as I talked and sobbed. Once I stopped to take a breath, he encouraged me to be with my tears and stay close to Larry's energy, to take comfort from it.

Pearl Harbor was somber, beautiful, and sacred. I watched tourists and soldiers touring the grounds. I recalled Paul Darling, my neighbor from childhood, who had served there. Had he been afraid when the Japanese bombed Pearl Harbor? More likely, he was brave and courageous. I heard a small voice inside myself respond, *That doesn't mean he wasn't scared.* I was scared and anxious of the days to come. How would I react at the funeral? What would it be like to meet and talk with the men who'd flown with Larry, men who were on the ground at his crash site after his plane went down? I knew what to do; I would draw on the strength of the Serenity Prayer. I would be courageous despite my fear.

Finally, it was time to leave Hawaii. We drove to the airport, where Doyle led the way to the gate. He stacked my over-packed briefcase, computer case, and purse onto a chair in the crowded waiting area as Laura and I sat down. Then he headed to the check-in desk to ask about watching the casket being placed into the plane. Three children chased one another up the aisle in front of us, providing a welcome diversion as I craned my head to see if Doyle was having any luck. As he talked to one of the ticketing agents, he pointed to Laura and me. Soon, he joined us again.

"She'll arrange for the two of you to go down to the runway. It will be just before the plane is ready to take off. You'll stay here until she's ready, and I'll take your things and wait for you by the boarding door. You'll have to have a security pass, and she'll have to get clearance. But don't worry. It will happen."

What would we have done without Doyle, I wondered. He didn't seem to care that I obsessed about the smallest things. He did his best to find a way to ease my concerns. We sat for over forty-five minutes. I was fidgety and uncomfortable, detached from Doyle and Laura. At times, I distracted myself by watching the children playing. The fact that Larry was going home, that he wasn't in the jungle anymore, was difficult for me to comprehend. Transporting him home was somehow disconcerting. I would no longer wonder where he was. I could sense a thirty-five-year-old era ending. But I was still afraid something would happen and he would be lost again. I told myself we were simply taking our last flight together. *Don't get crazy with this*, I chastised myself silently.

An attendant at the desk announced that they were ready to begin boarding. A second clerk headed for the door to take the boarding passes as passengers passed through to the jet way. I looked for the attendant whom Doyle had spoken to but couldn't see her. I began to panic. What if she'd left? I felt silly and stupid. I needed to see Larry's casket. Just then I looked up, startled, at the attendant standing right in front of us. "Put these on," she said to Laura and me. "They're your security passes."

Laura and I clipped the tags on our blouses.

"Follow me. We don't have much time. You can't actually go onto the runway." The attendant gave us instructions as we followed her at a brisk pace. "We don't have much time."

"My husband was killed in Laos during the Vietnam War," I announced. "They excavated his crash site this past July." I was out of breath from trying to keep up. The attendant stopped as we stepped onto the narrow sidewalk leading to the runway. As she turned and faced me, bright tears in her eyes gave me permission to cry, too. She hugged me, said she would pray for us, and told us where to stand.

The runway was a mass of confusing traffic. Drivers steered tractors pulling trailers loaded with luggage to the automated loading ramp that ran up into the plane's underbelly.

"I don't see him. Where is he?" I couldn't keep the pleading out of my voice.

The attendant steadied me by placing her hand on my arm as she explained, "Not to worry. He'll be the last cargo boarding."

"It would just be awful if he got misplaced," I whispered.

She pointed to a small tractor pulling a cart draped with plastic side panels. I couldn't see the casket inside.

"You can't step onto the runway, but the driver will bring it as close to you as he can. You'll be able to see it from here," the attendant assured me.

The driver stopped the cart twenty feet from where we stood. He jumped out and lifted the plastic curtain facing us to reveal a heavy cardboard carton. "Your husband's casket is inside," he explained. "The carton protects it in cargo."

Laura thanked him as her arm reached around my shoulders. Tears streamed down both our faces. Larry was coming home. We watched as the precious carton was loaded onto the ramp. Two baggage workers manually guided and held it secure until the casket was at a height impossible to reach from where they stood on the blacktop. One man patted the carton as it left his steadying hands. My heart flooded with appreciation at his simple gesture.

"We've got to move. The plane will be departing now. He was the last cargo to board." As the casket slipped inside the plane's belly, the attendant's firm instructions forced me to leave behind images of earlier times, when Larry had climbed into the cockpit to fly. The attendant moved us up the steps, through locked doors, and up more flights of stairs to the passenger waiting area, where

Doyle was standing with our belongings. He handed us our boarding passes as we hurried onto the ramp leading to the plane, and we were on our way. As the plane took off, I closed my eyes and imagined Larry not in the cargo but in the seat next to me on this last flight home.

THIRTY-ONE

A Promise Kept

Drizzly, dark skies welcomed us to Washington when we arrived on what was, ironically, Veteran's Day. When Doyle pulled up in front of the Doubletree Hotel, I saw my family sitting in the lobby through the glass entry doors. My eighty-four-year-old mother and her second husband, Leon, had come for the funeral. They were sitting with my brother's wife, Jeri. My brother had died nineteen years earlier, but I could feel him gathered there with the rest of my family. Having Jeri there was an immeasurable comfort. She had loved Larry and had traveled to Menninger with my brother and mother to be with me when Larry was killed.

It was so good to have them all with us.

I walked into the lobby and went straight to Mother. "Thanks for being here," I said, the tears starting again. When Mother had learned Larry's remains were coming home, she'd told me, "I prayed I'd be alive when Larry came home. I wish Mom and Dad Hull had lived long enough for this. I'll just have to represent his mother."

Leon, my stepdad, had known Larry when we first married and had attended Larry's first memorial service and met Larry's father, Chief Master Sergeant Robert J. Hull. He spoke of Larry now as if the return of his remains were personal.

School board members, principals, teachers, and friends, most from River Forest, were also waiting for us in the lobby. Overwhelmed with gratitude and touched by their support, I thanked them for coming and explained that Laura and I were exhausted and needed to freshen up. Our trip had begun to take its toll.

We joined Mother and Leon, Jeri, and her family for dinner at the hotel. Food was the last thing I wanted but I savored the time with my family. Mother and Leon, especially, were interested in the details of our trip to Hawaii.

Friends of Laura's had created a website announcing the recovery and return of Larry's remains and his funeral at Arlington. It included an itinerary of events to celebrate his life. Many of those present had learned about Larry and planned to attend his funeral because of the website. It was a beautiful and helpful way to honor Laura's father.

The next day, November 12, 2006, Laura and I were scheduled to welcome friends and family in the hospitality room at the hotel. I'd set my alarm for 5:30 a.m., but when it went off, I just couldn't get up. In the dark, I heard Laura say, "Mother, I'll go." I nodded a thank you as I lay back down, exhausted. My brain buzzed like a worn-out fluorescent bulb. "Just one more day; help me through one more day," I muttered before falling back to sleep.

Once I woke up for good, I lingered in bed. In some ways, it felt like Larry had died twice. The first time his remains were not returned, and I couldn't fully grieve. The second time was with the return of his remains, when we could and had to grieve. Larry really was gone, and we had to get this right. Many of the family and friends there for the service had their own personal demons and memories from "our war" to work through. Even friends of mine who were former Vietnam War protestors came to honor Larry, although they had never met him.

Larry's comrades who knew and loved him during flight training and in Vietnam also surrounded us. Many of them had attended a memorial service for him in Da Nang shortly after his plane went down in Laos, and they had longed for this day to come almost as much as I had. We all yearned to find a sense of peace and forgiveness, a healing of the bitterness we associated with the Vietnam War. Once more, Larry and the life he lived offered an opportunity for healing. I was so proud; Larry's homecoming would free more than just me.

As I stepped into the gathering a short while later, my eyes scanned the crowd. I noted a number of people I didn't recognize. A tall, graceful man moved toward me. "Tyra, I'm Cliff Newman, it's so good to meet you." He introduced himself as one of the Special Forces soldiers who'd worked with Larry. "Would you like to know how Larry was killed? I was there on the ground soon after his plane crashed."

My knees weakened. After all the years of imagining what had happened, I was about to hear the truth from someone who'd been there right after Larry died. "Yes," I said, "I want to know." I could no longer fall into the pit of despair of not knowing what had happened to Larry. I would know, and I would live with it gracefully. I could move on from this day.

Cliff's story was similar to Tom Yarborough's, with a few minor differences in the details. What mattered to me were not the minutiae of Larry's death but that someone was there at the crash site and could verify exactly what had happened. I made a point to introduce Cliff to Laura, so he could tell her how her father died, and also so she could visit with this wonderful man, who had come so far to tell us his story and honor her dad. Cliff was one of many that day for whom Laura and I were so very grateful.

We had hoped that anyone who came to celebrate Larry's life would leave having had the opportunity to heal some of the residual pain of the war. Now, I observed my daughter listening intently as men told stories about her dad. I watched her cry, laugh, and exhibit a kindness and gentleness toward them that filled me with pride. I watched as Vietnam veterans and war protestors shared the stories of their lives during the war. I was so grateful we had made the decision to share our family's experience of loss, strength, and hope. I knew Larry was pleased; I hadn't been able to find him on the beach in Hawaii, but I felt him there with me among those who had come to celebrate his life.

That evening, Laura and I moved into the restaurant to join some of our guests for dinner. I stepped out from the crowd to hug some friends and former school board members leaving with a school district entourage. When I took my arms from around the last one's neck and turned, I froze.

Susan stood in front of me. She had been at Larry's first memorial service in 1971. Including my mother, Leon, and my sister-in-law, she was one of only six people there who transcended the thirty-five-year time span between when we were informed Larry was missing and tomorrow's funeral.

I took Susan's face in my hands. "Is it you? It is you. Are you really here?" I sobbed. Susan and her husband had been in Florida when the guys were training on the Cessna O-2 before they left for Vietnam. She had been a nurse's aide and my friend. We'd met for dinner on a regular basis after our husbands left for Nam. We had feared for our husbands' lives, spent evenings together when I was lonely, terrified, and depressed. I had confided in her. She knew how much I had struggled and had encouraged me to go to Menninger. She had lost her husband too, when they divorced after he returned from Nam. There had been so many casualties of one kind or another. Susan's presence brought the 1971 loss and the 2006 loss together and diminished the sense that I was swinging between two worlds.

As I visited with friends and family, I wondered how the next day would go. Would the funeral I had promised Larry thirty-five years ago, when we were young newlyweds watching war movies, be all that he had imagined? Had he ever really believed that not coming home was a possibility? Did it seem plausible, given our belief, that he was answering a higher call? Perhaps it was just chatter on our part at the end of an emotionally charged war movie, as credits rolled over the screen to the tune of "God Bless America." In the movie, the hero's best friend had drawn the short straw and had to tell the young bride her first lieutenant was not coming home, ever.

Larry had made plans in the event that he did not come back. He'd bought a trailer house so Laura and I would have a place to live, and he'd purchased as much life insurance as he could afford. But he had not made plans or left instructions for coming home thirty-five years later in a box.

Boisterous laughter brought me back to the crowd around me. I knew that laugh. It was immediately familiar, yet I couldn't place it until Marty stepped in front of me, grinning sideways, his ears sticking straight out.

Marty had been Larry's best friend in college and the best man at our wedding. Could my heart be any fuller? Sadness and gratitude flooded my soul. Marty's presence was an abrupt reminder of the intense love affair between Larry and me. I had never known anyone who'd thought I was just right until Larry. Our first date had begun my real life fairy tale. Larry was the angel I had desperately prayed for when Daddy died. His soul and mine had connected immediately. In many ways, he'd never left me.

The night slipped by, and finally I turned to Laura. "I have to go to bed," I whispered. "Will you come with me to the room? Can we go now?" I was reminded of being a child and wishing I could be alone with my mother after my father died. I was struck by how much I depended on my daughter as she stood to accompany me to our room.

Conversation was minimal as we readied for bed, our funeral clothing already laid out. For the hundredth time, I checked to make sure I'd packed the pearls Larry had bought for me in Kobe, Japan. I'd worn them at his first memorial service, and I'd wear them at his funeral the next day.

THIRTY-TWO

Full Military Honors

The morning of Larry's funeral, I overslept. The date was November 13, 2006. The long and emotional journey had taken its toll. Over 150 people had come to welcome Larry home and lay him to rest; many of them were waiting for me downstairs. Just before I left the room, I clasped Larry's pearls around my neck. Tears sprang from in my eyes as I looked in the bathroom mirror and saw those gorgeous beads resting on my black dress. How strange it felt, to be fifty-nine years old, crying over losing my twenty-five-year-old Larry, and crying over never knowing him as he grew and matured. I couldn't imagine him at sixty-one. He would forever be twenty-five, and a part of me would stay twenty-four and never grow old. My life with Larry had ended when he died, but our spiritual connection continued. It always would. The past and present ran together. The circumstances felt so unusual and shocking. I was relieved to hear Larry's voice in my head, "Tyra, all you can do is your best. Just do your best."

The funeral procession followed the lead military car from the hotel to Arlington National Cemetery. The Rolling Thunder—a motley group of pony-tailed, Harley-riding veterans with hearts as big as Texas—and three flights of airmen stood at ease in formation in the parking lot in front of the Fort Myers Chapel. One flight carried rifles; another carried musical instruments.

Two groups of pilots had come to honor Larry. Some were the men who'd been in his pilot-training class at Reese Air Force Base in Lubbock. I remembered many of them and had played cards with some of their wives. The other group had been stationed with Larry at Da Nang. Some had flown secret missions in Prairie Fire with him. Others, Forward Air Controllers (FACS), flew with him over the Ho Chi Minh Trail at the beginning of his tour. Three Special Forces comrades had worked with Larry to plan and execute safe entry and exits behind enemy lines. They had been the boots on the ground around Larry's downed plane. They had known, depended on, and trusted Larry. I felt their love for Laura and me. I loved them all because they represented my husband. I shut my eyes, and my mind filled with Larry, grinning at me as always, and saying, "We done good, honey, we done good. These are my guys. Aren't they great?"

I leaned out the open window of the limo. Tom had told me that Larry would have a caisson just like President John F. Kennedy, except for the riderless horse. I choked at the sight of the white horses harnessed to the caisson parked in front of the chapel. After the service, the horses would take Larry to his resting place.

Doyle escorted Laura and me in to meet the chaplain. We signed documents indicating that I would be buried with Larry when I needed my own place. I had thought long and hard about that decision. Since I had divorced Kenneth, I was still considered an unmarried widow. As long as I stayed unmarried, I would meet the qualifications for burial at Arlington.

A young marine stepped into the room, took Laura's arm, and guided her toward the door. As Larry's daughter, she was officially the next of kin. I cringed. Would I have to walk alone into my husband's funeral? To my relief, Laura took my arm in hers, and the three of us walked into the chapel. "How Great Thou Art" hummed softly from the pipe organ as I took my place between Mother and Laura. Six uniformed soldiers brought Larry's flag-draped casket forward as we rose and stood at attention.

My youthful husband's handsome face looked up at me from the front of the funeral program.

As I listened to Tom Yarborough's eulogy, I thought about the first time I'd met him, back on Memorial Day weekend in 1994, when Laura and I had gone to Washington to see the Vietnam Memorial. Tom had become a friend and my lifeline back to Larry's time in Vietnam. That day, he read a tribute he'd written for Larry and the men who had flown with him. Tom was poetic and gracious. He honored those who lived and those who had died. He too had promised himself that he would see Larry's remains returned to American soil. The funeral gave many of us the opportunity to tell ourselves we had done all that we could do for ourselves, each other, and, most importantly, for Larry.

The organist played "Amazing Grace" as Tom stepped down from the pulpit. The notes reverberated up my spine. In my mind's eye, I visualized Larry chasing me around the kitchen table, laughing and teasing. "Girl, I'm going to tickle you! You're going to laugh 'til you cry, pumpkin. You're it. I got you. Now laugh until you cry or I'll tickle you more. . . . Laugh until you cry. You hear me? Laugh 'til you cry now."

Inside I wailed, *I want you back, Larry! Damn it, why did you go and get killed? I wanted you home years ago. Not in a box. Not thirty-five years later.*

I stood up to say the Lord's Prayer, then a short while later, eased out of the pew and took Doyle's arm. We followed Laura and her young marine escort as they walked out behind Larry's flag-draped coffin, then we watched as six uniformed soldiers hoisted his casket onto the caisson. I was sorry Larry's mother and father were not there to witness this honorable tribute to their son. I hoped they were with Larry, watching and full of pride.

Larry's comrades followed on foot behind the soldier bearing the POW/MIA flag. The flag bearer followed the caisson. He would remain nearby until Larry's coffin was lowered into the ground and stay on guard afterward. His presence was reassuring. He was there to ensure that this soldier, once missing in action, was laid in his final resting place, never to be disturbed again.

How long had I mourned Larry? Had I ever stopped since the day he'd left for Vietnam? I wanted it to end, and yet I feared it would do just that. There would be no more of First Lt. James Larry Hull once he was laid to rest.

In 1971, seven Honor Guard airmen honored my husband with the three-volley salute at the cemetery in my hometown after the memorial service. I had hoped and prayed even then that one day Larry would have a real funeral at Arlington. Now, as we stepped toward the chairs set up graveside, I saw Larry's casket. It would not be long before he was lowered into the ground. It seemed like we'd had so little time with him, and yet I knew we had to put an end to this strange half-life we had been left with after his plane went down in the Laotian jungle. The chaplain finished his remarks, the band played "Amazing Grace" again, and in Larry's honor, twenty-one blanks tore through the damp, overcast sky. The explosion from the rifles punctuated an eerie silence. "Taps" played, solemn, prayerful, and holy.

The Honor Guard began the lovely ritual of folding the flag that had been draped over the coffin. It was a long and slow process. Someone had told me the honor was in the precision. With each fold, the flag snapped a crisp salute, and another image of Larry appeared in my memory. Scenes of my life with him played like a home movie in my mind. In one, Laura, Larry, and I played in the sand in Ft. Walton Beach, Florida. I heard myself squeal, "Why do you tickle me all the time? You never stop!"

"That's easy," Larry giggled, "so I can hear you laugh. Tyra, try to have faith. Don't worry, Tyra. Please don't cry. I'll be home, I promise."

Finally, the flag was folded and given to a young colonel. With solemnity and graciousness, he presented the flag to Laura and expressed his condolences to both of us. Laura and I stepped up to the casket to scatter white rose petals over Larry's coffin. His comrades followed with nickels, and members of The Rolling Thunder left beads strung on leather bands, representing the Vietnam Service Medal and the Vietnam Campaign Medal.

After the burial, we gathered for a reception at the Women's Memorial. A harpist played sixties and seventies music, including "Bridge Over Troubled Water," released in 1970. Slides of Larry that had been converted to video played nonstop. We ate the food I'd had catered, and we visited. We took photographs to ensure that we remembered the occasion. We laughed and cried and visited some more. For thirty-five years I had thought it would never be over. I could still hardly believe it really was complete.

~~~~~

Laura and I had an extra day in Washington after Larry's funeral. She woke me early that morning. "Mother, we have a mission," she announced. Tears welled up in her eyes. "I've been wanting to do this for years. I have one of Daddy's funeral programs. We're going to go to Arlington and be at the grave, just the three of us, before you and I have to go back to Chicago. Then we'll stop at The Wall. We'll lean the program against The Wall so everyone can see it. They'll know my dad, First Lt. James L. Hull, is finally home, and he's buried at Arlington National Cemetery, just like he wanted."

As our cab pulled up to the hotel, Laura asked me, "Did you see a Washington paper yesterday?"

Before I could answer, she continued, "Did you hear anyone say if Dad's photo and the story about his funeral were in the paper?"

I shook my head no.

"It's too bad," Laura said. "The story was in papers all over. You'd think it would have been in the ones here."

"Beautiful day today, yes?" The cabbie smiled widely and peeked at us in the rearview mirror as we climbed into the cab. "Where to?" he asked.

"Arlington National Cemetery," Laura replied.

We rode for a while in silence, then the cabbie said, "There was a pilot buried at Arlington yesterday. He was killed years ago. Did you hear about that?"

"It might have been my dad," Laura answered. "Did you see yesterday's paper?" she asked the driver as he pulled up to the curb alongside Larry's grave.

The driver said, "Normally, every morning when I get in my cab, I drive to Dunkin' Donuts for coffee and a donut. I throw away yesterday's paper and buy a new paper. For some reason, I didn't throw yesterday's paper away this morning." He reached over and picked up a folded *Washington Times* from the console between his front seats.

Shaking the paper out to full size, he pointed to the familiar handsome pilot in official dress uniform. The photo was a copy of the one we'd used on the funeral program. The driver pointed to the headline of the article: "Thirty-five-year odyssey ends with Arlington burial, pilot's body returned from Laos." Three sets of eyes watered as our cabbie opened the door for us. "Don't worry," he assured us. "I'll wait as long as you want.

Afterward, our cabbie drove us to The Vietnam Memorial Wall. We walked arm in arm up to the sleek black memorial. Tears of relief and exhaustion from our ten-day journey flowed.

"Larry, you were and are loved. The love and miracles have been amazing because of you," I said.

Laura slipped her arm out of mine, bent down, and laid Larry's funeral program below his name on the sidewalk at the base of The Wall.

"He's home," our beloved daughter said. "It's finished."

EPILOGUE

Spring arrived about six months after we buried Larry. The daffo-
dils in my backyard began to peek through the mulch. The funeral
director at Arlington Cemetery had assured Laura and me that
Larry's marker would be installed as soon as the ground thawed.
I wanted very badly to go see it, but each time I mentioned a trip
to DC to Laura, we'd both bemoan our overscheduled calendars.
When I got the opportunity to attend a conference in Washington
in April 2007, it felt like the hand of fate.

Tom Yarborough accompanied me to the cemetery early on a
Saturday morning. He had become a mainstay in our lives. Our
bond was Larry. Tom occasionally voiced the same kind of guilt I
often felt—guilt over surviving, of not doing enough for Larry, of
not protecting him or bringing him home sooner. I confessed to
Tom that I'd worried for years that my illness had distracted Larry
and caused him to lose his concentration when he flew, resulting
in his death.

As Tom and I walked through the aisles, we were disoriented
about where Larry's grave was located. He had been buried last on
his row, which had been the one closest to the street. But there
had been so many burials since his funeral that now that was no
longer the case. We separated and walked back and forth down
rows among the November death dates, where we thought Larry
should have been, since graves were lined up in consecutive order
by death dates.

Soon, we found ourselves in the December rows. Frustrated I blurted out, "Tom, wouldn't you know we'd lose him again? How can this be? I know he's in section sixty-six in the Iraqi Section. He's the only Vietnam guy in the Iraqi Section."

As I complained to Tom about not being able to find Larry, I focused on a white marker sitting crooked in the grass in a cocky sort of way: JAMES L. HULL, 1st LT, US AIR FORCE, VIETNAM, DEC 28, 1945, FEB 19, 1971, SILVER STAR, DFC & OLC, PURPLE HEART, AM & 8 OLC.

The February death date had not registered in either of our minds. We had acted as if Larry had died in November 2006, when we buried him. Tom and I had both walked by his grave several times but hadn't seen it. We'd never have found him if his marker hadn't been crooked. From six feet below ground, Larry was still teasing. It was just like my fun-loving husband to hide from us in full sight.

Tom and I went for coffee afterwards and lamented over the number of graves that had been added for soldiers from the Iraq and Afghanistan conflicts. Then we turned our attention back to Larry and shared stories about him.

That day, I was proud. Proud of Larry's service, proud that he laid in peace among his fellow heroes, and proud of our country for keeping its promise to never forget our fallen soldiers. Most of all, I felt grateful that James L. Hull had never left me. His spirit is forever with me. Flesh and bones may die, but loving relationships never do.

AUTHOR Q&A

1. *What inspired you to write a memoir about Larry and your time at the Menninger Clinic, and what message do you want readers to take away from* Where the Water Meets the Sand?

Where the Water Meets the Sand is a love gift to Larry and the men and women who gave their lives both literally and figuratively in the divisive war in Vietnam. Some veterans physically came home, but many continue to suffer the effects of PTSD, addiction, and mental illness, as do their loved ones.

The inspiration for my book has always been to highlight the struggles of families who lose loved ones in war. But all of us lose people we love in one way or another. While my memoir doesn't soft-pedal the trials and challenges of living in the aftermath of horrific losses, depression, or addiction, it emphasizes that we can move forward. Mine is a story of hope, of believing there is a power greater than any of us that can help us heal if we are willing to embrace the opportunities placed in our path. Throughout my life that spiritual power has provided people who helped me and believed in me.

2. *You are very candid about your struggle with depression and addiction. What was it like for you to revisit so many painful memories and experiences as you wrote this memoir?*

I am who I am because of my life experiences. Over the years I've become more accepting of my illness and appreciative of my recovery. As I revisited painful experiences through the very therapeutic process of writing, I felt ashamed and disappointed that I hadn't handled some situations differently, such as becoming pregnant as a teenager, and when I grew so overcome with fear and depression that I realized I was addicted to alcohol. There were many times while writing this book when I relived the devastation of my father's early death, the desperation of my adolescence, and my confusion, hopelessness, and fear of losing Larry. The salve was that I reached out for help, and there was always someone there to help me. *Always.* This is one of the most important things I realized yet again from writing my story: I was so taken care of, even when I couldn't take care of myself.

A willingness and openness to seek help and accept treatment is crucial. For some family members or friends, the person they care about may not be aware of their own need or may be unwilling to receive help. Some people I met in the hospital psychiatric unit in Lubbock, Texas, at Menninger, and in addiction support groups received help because someone had intervened on their behalf. I've known others who've tried to help but were unsuccessful. They too may need support. But the stigma and lack of empathy toward those who require treatment is still a gigantic hurdle. As a result, many of us discuss our own struggles and those of the ones we love in whispers, and we keep our illnesses secret, perpetuating the barrier to treatment. Access to first class, affordable treatment and the knowledge of where to find it is still a challenge. Having said that, there are resources for those who seek help if we persevere.

3. *Can you share a little about your writing process? For example, is there anything special that you do, such as keeping journals, writing at a scheduled time, or attending writer's groups?*

I have attended writers' groups from time to time. I sought the support of writing coaches. I did a writer's residency at Ragdale in Lake Forest, Illinois, which helped me believe I was a writer and that what I had to say mattered. I also took my first writing workshop at Ragdale. Whenever I got discouraged about the book throughout the years it took me to write it, I'd hear the voice of one of my fellow workshop participants who'd said to me after I read an excerpt aloud in the workshop, "Keep writing. You have a gift and it's a sin to waste it."

Unlike some writers, I don't write at a certain time or write a specific number of hours or pages each day. Over the years when I missed Larry terribly, I unpacked his olive brown suitcase where I kept Air Force documents regarding his MIA/KIA case and went through them. It made me feel closer to him. My writing process has been a similar unpacking process. I started the memoir in 1984 and worked on it sporadically, in fits and starts. While I was still working in education, it was difficult to immerse myself in the past and live in the present simultaneously. Once I retired, meditation and surrounding myself with music, often Larry's recorded music from Vietnam, were catalysts to finding a rhythm and cadence for writing my story.

4. *Where the Water Meets the Sand is such a beautiful title that evokes lovely poetic imagery. You mention it a few times in the book. Can*

you talk a bit more about your inspiration for the title and how you came up with it?

Where the Water Meets the Sand was the title from the moment I made the decision to write my memoir. Before Larry left for Vietnam, we dreamt of meeting on the beach in Hawaii. Some of my favorite memories with my husband took place near the water, such as the time he took me crabbing off the pier in Mobile, Alabama, and our ritual during Larry's training in Florida, when we'd sit on the pier trailing our feet over the waves splashing below.

When Larry died, I promised I'd always meet him on the beach in Hawaii where the water meets the sand. Throughout my life whenever I missed him or needed to make a decision regarding raising our daughter, I'd meet Larry there in my mind. Eerily enough, although not all that surprising to me, when Larry's remains were found and Laura and I went to Hawaii to escort him to Arlington, our hotel was right on the beach, where the water meets the sand.

5. *Your journey of recovery from depression and self-harm is inspiring and courageous. When did you first know that you needed professional help? And what gave you the courage to seek it out?*

I realized as a teenager that my other friends didn't drink like I did—alone and on weekdays. I often took beer and sat near my father's grave, on a bench engraved with our last name, Decker. I went there to talk with Daddy. I kept my talks with him a secret from everyone else. I knew my drinking was out of control, but as a teenager I didn't know what to do about it, nor did I understand the impact on my life. I didn't want to give it up. It kept me from feeling the overwhelming sadness. Later, binging and purging and cutting fulfilled the same need. With Larry, I felt safe. He accepted me and loved me unconditionally. I realized that I was in trouble and needed help when Larry left to train on the plane he would fly in Vietnam. His departure to Florida turned on a steady deafening drumbeat in my head. *What if he didn't come home?* I was so depressed that I couldn't take care of Laura or manage simple daily functions. I was ashamed and knew I needed help. My dependence on Larry for my wellbeing made it impossible to live with the raging fear that he might not come home once he left for Vietnam.

I don't think my decision to go to Menninger was courageous. It was a necessity, not a choice. I wasn't able to take care of myself, much less Laura, and I was afraid.

6. *You met many interesting people at the Menninger Clinic and formed some valuable friendships while you were there. Have you maintained any of those relationships throughout your life? If so, can you speak a little about that?*

I maintained friendships with other patients for a while after I left the Clinic. Since I was in outpatient therapy on the Menninger campus, I often joined my friends who still lived at the hospital for lunch or dinner in the dining room. Some of my friends came with me to the award ceremony at Forbes Air Force base when Larry's medals were awarded to me. Mrs. Locke and I also maintained a relationship once I left the hospital. I adored her.

I earned my Master's degree and graduated from KU. As I made my way along the traditional walk for graduates through the Campanile, Dr. Roberts stepped out from the crowd of well-wishers lining our path and reached out his hand. Taking mine, he said, "Good job. You should be proud." It was a gift I'll carry with me forever. It was the last time I saw him. On the first day of classes in my new job as principal of Boswell Junior High School, my social worker, analyst, and aides on my unit at Menninger brought their children to school to enroll. I was frantic at first, but my fears eased when I learned they were happy to see me. I had my own private cheering section, and I knew they were proud of my accomplishments.

7. *What do you do today to maintain your recovery?*

I meditate. I say the Serenity Prayer five times out loud every morning and every night. It is my mantra. I say it and thank God for my grandmother Nennie. I treasure my daughter and thank Larry and God for her love and friendship. I don't spend too much time alone, but rather spend quality time with other people. My closest friends are supportive and allow me to do the same for them. I never forget where I've been, and I remember that I am never alone. I believe and know that nothing is the end of the world, that all things are opportunities for growth. I volunteer on children's behalf, I love to be outdoors, and I spend wonderful time with my Border Collie mix, Bella.

Since coming back to Texas, I've forged new and lovely relationships with my mother and my sister. For that I am grateful. My addictions have not been active for years, and I will celebrate thirty-five years of sobriety on July 1, 2016, one day at a time. I am devoting my energy to bringing messages of hope to those experiencing mental health issues and to the people who love them. I've experienced a sense of joy and deep satisfaction through giving to others. That helps keep me healthy.

8. *You are very accomplished, and you did it as a single mother in the seventies and eighties. There were other wives and children who were struggling with the same tragedies, but it must have been very*

hard. What are some of the struggles you faced as a single mother at that time?

My second husband loved Laura and was an excellent father figure. He cared for her while I worked and went to school and taught her valuable life lessons. For that reason, it would be disingenuous for me to describe my life at that time as being a single mother.

After our divorce, I faced the trials and challenges of single parenthood. By then, Laura was becoming a teenager. She grew interested in knowing more about Larry. There were so few stories to tell since she was two years old when he was killed. I tried hard to do things with her to make up for her loss, but given the loss of my own father, I knew no one could make up for that. It tormented me at times. Throughout her childhood and young adulthood, I struggled to make up for the loss of her father. Of course it was impossible.

When Laura earned her driver's license, I felt traumatized when she left the house in the car I had bought for her. Because of my car accident and my irresponsibility as a teenager, I worried that she would have an accident and be severely injured. It was hard not to project my past behavior onto her. I received a call at work in Highland Park when she was sixteen. A glass company's van had crashed into her car after running a stop sign. The RN in the emergency room called to tell me but insisted Laura would be fine. I was frantic. Laura had told her I would be and cautioned her not to upset me. When I saw the huge gash across her forehead, I fainted. The thought of losing Laura is impossible to describe even now. When she chose a college on the east coast, I was devastated but didn't tell her. Just as I didn't tell Larry how overwrought I was when he fulfilled his dream of flying in Vietnam, I didn't tell Laura how much I hated for her to go so far away. Her dreams and education were too important for me to interfere. Throughout her life when I struggled about significant decisions that had to be made, I'd meet Larry on the beach at the water's edge and relied on his counsel.

9. *Military families coping with the stresses of deployment—the absence, injury, or illness of a loved one—likely will gain comfort from the fact that you are able to thrive both personally and professionally after years of suffering from depression and grief. What role did the military play in enabling and/or supporting your recovery?*

I could never have afforded treatment at the Menninger Clinic had it not been for the military insurance our family received. From that perspective, I often say, "Larry Hull saved my life. Not only did he love me for who I was, without him, I could never have gone to Menninger for treatment." There was an air force sergeant assigned to me after Larry's death. Many of the tasks he helped me accomplish were priceless: making arrangements for veterans benefits, getting a social security card and a military identification card so I could shop at the Forbes Air Force Base exchange and commissary after I left the hospital, taking me to the bank to deposit the life insurance checks that had been delivered to me at the Clinic by the USAA representative, and introducing me to the director of the daycare facility on base so that I could consider it for Laura when she came to live with me.

Sgt. Hanks and later Nat Hernandez at the Mortuary Division at Randolph Air Force Base in San Antonio, Texas, became my lifeline to the real possibility that Larry would one day come home.

Nat and one of his colleagues flew to Highland Park, Illinois, to meet with Laura and me. The four of us planned Larry's funeral in my living room as if we were all family. In a way, we were. We met Doyle, our personal escort, in Hawaii. He took us to JPAC to view and accept Larry's bones, to the funeral home to see the casket, and he escorted all three of us back to Washington for Larry's funeral. Doyle never left our side until the funeral and reception were over. We were his last case before his retirement.

10. *Receiving Larry's remains after so many years was obviously a very emotional time for you. What was it like to finally have closure and to be able to put him to rest at Arlington like you promised?*

"Closure" doesn't begin to express the miracle of Larry's remains coming home. When he was buried at Arlington, my sense of peace was complete, not like when we held his first memorial service. I felt empty and incomplete when that service was over, as if we had performed a perfunctory requirement. I wanted Larry to have a real service like my father had. I had kissed Daddy when he died, I had told him good-bye. Larry's memorial service didn't satisfy that need.

In spite of the odds, somewhere in my soul a tiny voice assured me that one day Larry's remains would come home to American soil and he would be buried at Arlington as I had promised. Seeing and touching Larry's bones in Hawaii at the JPAC lab was a mystical experience. It was as if a surge of electricity moved through my body when I pressed my hands down on his bones. I knew at that moment I touched him that he was present, with us. For me, it was not closure. It was a promise kept.

At the very beginning of the book, we know that Larry is about to leave for Vietnam. What does Tyra's reaction to his leaving reveal about her personality? Does the fact that she lost her father as a child make his leaving even harder for her?

Contrast how Tyra's experience as a single mother in the seventies and eighties might differ from a single mother's today. Considering these differences, was it harder for her to accomplish her successes and achievements?

What was the catalyst in Tyra's determination to survive? Was there one experience in particular that you felt was the turning point?

Having the self-awareness to understand that she needed to leave her daughter with a caretaker while she got treatment was an admirable thing for Tyra to do. What does this self-awareness in the midst of such severe depression say about Tyra's strength of character?

Dr. Roberts was a valuable asset in Tyra's recovery. What do we know about Dr. Roberts from the book? How would you describe his therapeutic approach? What was it about his personality and manner that worked so well with Tyra and made them such a great doctor/patient team?

Tyra's fellow patients in the Menninger Clinic were a support system for her. Discuss some of these characters (e.g., Mrs. Locke, The Minister, George, Deborah) and in what ways they helped Tyra. How did Emily and Trudi contribute to Tyra's sense of belonging?

Unfortunately, Tyra's experience of losing her husband in Vietnam was not unique. Should Tyra be considered "lucky," because she was able to finally bury Larry?

Larry's voice is a prominent figure in Tyra's inner reflection. The reader comes to know him through Tyra. What do we know about Larry because of this?

The Vietnam Conflict created a great amount of strife between the citizens of our country. Discuss how hard it must have been for Tyra and others like her, who lost their husbands, sons, and brothers in a war that many Americans did not support.

ABOUT THE AUTHOR

Photo by Karen Quiroz

Dr. Tyra Manning's story is both unique and universal, as it demonstrates the pervasive devastation of loss while demonstrating how courage and love can triumph. Tyra's husband was shot down over the Laotian jungle while flying a top-secret mission during the Vietnam War. She learned of his death while she was hospitalized at the Menninger Clinic where she was being treated for depression. Tyra's worst fear had come true.

Determined to fulfill the rest of the dreams and promises she and her husband had made to one another, that she get well and become a teacher, Dr. Manning persevered through the darkest of times, ultimately earning a doctorate in education from the University of Kansas and becoming one of the nation's top school superintendents. She has devoted her forty-year career to helping children achieve their highest potential. Since retiring in 2004, Dr. Manning's mission has been to share her personal journey of hope with individuals experiencing depression, addiction, and loss, and the people who love them.

Though she travels around the country delivering the messages and lessons in her new book, *Where the Water Meets the Sand*, Dr. Manning is a born and bred Texan. She currently resides in the Texas Hill Country with her border collie mix, Bella.